Mental Toughness

Everyday Habits to Build Mental Resilience and Achieve Success

Luke Thybulle

Luke Thybulle

© Copyright 2023 - All rights reserved.

The content contained within this book may not be reproduced, duplicated or transmitted without direct written permission from the author or the publisher.

Under no circumstances will any blame or legal responsibility be held against the publisher, or author, for any damages, reparation, or monetary loss due to the information contained within this book, either directly or indirectly.

Legal Notice:

This book is copyright protected. It is only for personal use. You cannot amend, distribute, sell, use, quote or paraphrase any part, or the content within this book, without the consent of the author or publisher.

Disclaimer Notice:

Please note the information contained within this document is for educational and entertainment purposes only. All effort has been executed to present accurate, up to date, reliable, complete information. No warranties of any kind are declared or implied. Readers acknowledge that the author is not engaged in the rendering of legal, financial, medical or professional advice. The content within this book has been derived from various sources. Please consult a licensed professional before attempting any techniques outlined in this book.

By reading this document, the reader agrees that under no circumstances is the author responsible for any losses, direct or indirect, that are incurred as a result of the use of the information contained within this document, including, but not limited to, errors, omissions, or inaccuracies.

Luke Thybulle

Table of Contents

Table of Contents 5
Introduction 7
Chapter 1: Introduction to Mental Toughness 13
   An Overview 14
   Why It's Important to Be Mentally Tough 19
   Everyday Habits for Building Mental Toughness 23
Chapter 2: Understanding Mental Resilience 33
   Understanding the Concept of Resilience 33
   How Mental Resilience Is Related to Mental Toughness 37
   The Pillars of Mental Resilience 41
   Everyday Habits for Building Mental Resilience 45
Chapter 3: Stop Limiting Yourself and Start Growing! 51
   Understanding Limiting Beliefs 52
   Techniques for Overcoming Limiting Beliefs 56
   A Growth Mindset 61
   Everyday Habits for Building a Growth Mindset 62
Chapter 4: Building a Positive Mindset 67
   The Effects of Positive Thinking 67
   Recognizing Negative Thinking Patterns 71
   Everyday Habits for Building a Positive Mindset 78
Chapter 5: Setting Realistic and Achievable Goals 85
   The Importance of Goal Setting 87
   How to Set Effective and Achievable Goals 90

How to Create a Plan for Achieving Your Goals 95

Everyday Habits for Achieving Your Goals 100

Chapter 6: Building Emotional Intelligence............. 103

Understanding Emotional Intelligence 103

How Emotional Intelligence Relates to Mental Toughness . 109

Everyday Habits for Building Emotional Intelligence 117

Chapter 7: Managing Stress and Emotions 123

Understanding the Effects of Stress on Mental Toughness . 124

Everyday Habits for Managing Stress 128

Everyday Habits for Regulating Your Emotions 133

Chapter 8: Harnessing the Power of Self-Talk 145

The Impact of Self-Talk on Mental Toughness 146

How to Change Negative Self-Talk to Positive Self-Talk 149

Everyday Habits for Effective Self-Talk 152

Conclusion 157

References 1657

Introduction

The adage "bloom where you're planted" exhorts people to seize chances, value their current circumstances, and succeed despite them. But, in practice, when they are not happy with their current circumstances, many people find it difficult to maintain this mindset. Nonetheless, there are several strategies to cultivate a positive outlook and utilize one's resources.

Realizing that you have control over your thoughts is the first step. Thoughts are frequently assumed to be outside of our control, but attitudes are something we can manage. We influence how we decide to interpret the events taking place around us in any particular circumstance. Consider focusing on other positive elements of your life, for example, seeing your current job as a stepping stone to your dream job, or using your dissatisfaction as motivation to work harder if you are unhappy with your current employment. Use resources, tools, and prospects, and profit from networking possibilities.

It's crucial to keep your thoughts under control because they have a big impact on your mindset. Decide to find the silver lining in every circumstance and cultivate gratitude for what you have. Change the way you think about the negative things and try to see the good in everything. The caliber of your thinking determines how happy your life will be.

Life is full of change, oftentimes in a manner that is unfavorable to us. Therefore, to thrive even in unfavorable conditions, we must learn to accept it. We can improve mental flexibility by learning to accept change, which aids in adapting to new situations, being open-minded, and spotting chances that can significantly alter a situation. One can advance in life by learning to adapt rather than being disturbed by change, which is necessary for personal growth.

Change is inescapable, and how we react to it determines how successful we are. Your creativity and passion are the only constraints on your effectiveness. Find the opportunities that change brings rather than becoming afraid of it. Accept new difficulties and experiences and learn from them.

Choose not to let challenging times define you because not everything that happens to you is under your control. It is crucial to focus on the good things in your life if you want to flourish where you are planted. Your energy may decrease as a result of a pessimistic mindset, and it can be challenging to adopt a positive outlook. Try to cherish and enjoy what you have right now rather than dwelling on a perfect circumstance. Make an effort to enjoy the relationships, activities, or personal accomplishments that bring you happiness, by concentrating on them. It's easy to fixate on what you don't have, but it's essential to value what you do.

Let go of negative thoughts and emotions and place your focus on the activities, people, and relationships that are joyous, and remember that there are lessons to be learned in each situation. This can be done by transforming difficult circumstances into worthwhile learning opportunities by finding life lessons in them. Regardless of the challenge, always seek the positive aspects of it. You can gain knowledge about resiliency, self-discovery, or how to choose wisely in the future. If you are unable to see the lessons right away, assure yourself that you will eventually learn something because every event offers a chance to develop and learn.

Even if you feel close to defeat, there are treasures to be found. By taking the time to learn from your experiences, you place yourself in a better position to make more informed decisions in the future. The practice of acknowledging and embracing your present predicament, even what you cannot change, is known as *radical acceptance*. This way of thinking is all about accepting your current situation, with all of its ups and downs, and not dwelling on hypothetical possibilities.

Radical acceptance is realizing that pain is not necessary and does not entail accepting the current status quo. You have a choice in how you react to and understand the circumstance. Inconveniences such as traffic or not being promoted at your workplace not only make you realize that everything happens for a reason, they also develop your ability to tolerate greater setbacks.

Accepting your current situation as it is and putting your attention on what you can affect are two aspects of radical acceptance. We are forced to change ourselves when we can no longer affect a situation. Focus on making constructive changes where you can while practicing accepting what you cannot. It's critical to pinpoint places where you can implement changes to enhance your current condition.

Complaining about unpleasant conditions does not bring about change, on the contrary, it might be detrimental to your wellbeing. Instead, try to maximize the current circumstances, endeavor to change what you can, and take chances to meet new people and investigate new opportunities.

"Bloom where you're planted" refers to the idea of maximizing the chances that come our way, appreciating the current position, and thriving despite the conditions. Having a positive outlook gives us the ability to take advantage of the chances and circumstances we are in. This entails embracing change, paying attention to life's benefits, learning from your experiences, appreciating what you already have, engaging in radical acceptance, and figuring out how to enhance your current circumstances.

No matter where you land, we can all grow and thrive by cultivating the appropriate mindset.

It comes as no surprise that you need mental toughness to bloom where you are planted. People are too often discouraged when it seems that things don't go as planned or expected. Sometimes, these things pass, and the only thing that was required to thrive was resilience. In this book, *Mental Toughness*, we will look at tips, tools, and strategies you can implement to thrive where you are.

Imagine that your happiness won't depend on favorable circumstances. Imagine that your success won't depend on things "going your way". Let's be honest—life happens! We can predict, expect, and plan, but every so often, life will throw us a curveball. All we need to do is learn how to catch it. And *that* is the purpose of this book.

We'll discuss mental toughness and why it is essential to thriving. We'll talk about habits you can cultivate to establish, build, and maintain mental toughness. We'll also talk about mental resilience and how it relates to mental toughness. Then, we'll see how mental resilience is shaped.

We'll examine mindsets and how they can affect your life. We'll discuss the importance of having a growth mindset, and how you cultivate the need for this mindset. We'll examine how you can turn negative thinking patterns into positive ones. Negative thinking patterns can be detrimental to your success; therefore, it is essential to dig deep and rewire our brains where necessary.

We'll talk about goal setting and the importance of realistic goals, as well as the power of emotional intelligence. We'll then examine the effects of stress on mental toughness, and how to successfully handle stress. We'll look at the power of positive self-talk and see how different manners of self-talk affect us.

Are you ready to bloom where you are planted? Do you hunger for the skills to thrive in whatever circumstance you may find yourself in? Just remember—you are not alone in your struggles. Many others, including myself, had to learn how to change, accept, adapt, and build a tough mindset to thrive where we would've previously wilted. But now, we have the opportunity to stand strong and face any circumstance, smiling, and knowing that we'll do more than survive—we'll thrive!

FREE E-Book: Discover How to Finally Conquer Your Fears

PLUS I'll share with you
My #1 Secret To Guaranteed Success...
See firsthand how I direct my focus to live a life full of energy, passion and confidence.

- Luke Thybulle

www.northstarreaders.com/luke-thybulle/conquer-your-fears

Chapter 1: Introduction to Mental Toughness

People competing for pure enjoyment, leisure, and innocent recreation are uncommon in today's environment. The catchphrase "it does not matter whether we win or lose" is becoming less and less common and is considered outdated. The urge and drive to win seem to be increasingly prevalent in the world that we live in today. Perhaps, what is alluring and encapsulates our desire for success is the idea of becoming the best, the most powerful, or the most intelligent. The desire to excel, or at the very least to constantly improve, permeates nearly every endeavor that humanity undertakes.

Let's look at an example. What distinguishes an athlete who thrives in a top league from one who crumbles under pressure? Why is it that certain athletes can overcome extreme hardship while others are unable to? Why do some athletes have the ability to withstand and ignore adverse effects during competition while others allow them to affect and detract them from their competitive performance? What enables athletes to bounce back after losing and experiencing failure on a personal level?

Perhaps the successful development, application, and ongoing maintenance of mental toughness hold the answers to these questions.

Today's top athletes understand that winning involves more than technique and extends to a new area known as the "psychology of winning," which encompasses a variety of different mental components like context-specific mental skills found in programs designed for mental toughness.

An Overview

Research into the phenomena of mental toughness was previously hampered by the widely-held belief that it was nothing more than a big cliché. The phrase *mental toughness* is one of the least understood and has been the subject of much debate among researchers (Pattison, 2013). Today's circumstances are a little different. The idea of mental toughness is no longer new or strange, and the growing amount of scholarly research on the phenomenon plainly demonstrates the significance and value that many people attach to it.

Currently, psychological influences on performance are growing more significant and vital, to the point that many individuals understand that success cannot be assured by skills alone. In reality, several researchers have identified mental toughness as a key determinant in achieving performance excellence and as a performance booster. Although numerous researchers support this viewpoint, there is still a worrying lack of acceptance of the influence of psychological intervention and its effects on performance.

Researchers are still attempting to win over a somewhat resistant audience for their studies using the mental toughness and psychological intervention frameworks.

Our capacity to effectively balance internal and external demands will determine whether we experience positive or negative emotional reactions in response to stressful situations or other types of adversity, as well as the implications these reactions have on our productivity. This is the capacity to access the mental side of performance optimization and enhancement, which is moving beyond pure physical aptitude, skill, and ability.

Too many people ignore mental aspects of productivity when faced with challenges, and whenever they are put in situations that call for higher levels of performance, their first instinct is usually to adjust all levels and phases of their training and development before the mental aspect of productivity is even taken into account.

Understand that mental toughness is essential in every aspect of life—the corporate world, family life, sports, and anything else you can think of that may require a lot of mental effort. As I stated, people often underestimate the value of being mentally tough. Think about it this way: Sometimes we believe we are capable of handling anything life throws at us. Then, sometimes, even the tiniest setback can feel overwhelming. Wherein lies the difference?

Our response is not always based on the situation we find ourselves in. Many of us have experienced being upset by something that normally wouldn't bother us. Then, it's easy for us to dismiss huge disappointments as inevitable aspects of life.

It's not what's happening that makes a difference; it's our mental toughness. We can fend off negative thoughts by using our mental strength. It enables us to daily reenter the ups and downs of life. It's a kind of mental muscle that we may build to enhance our general well-being, just like exercising muscles for physical strength.

Luke Thybulle

What Mental Toughness Isn't

First of all, mental toughness isn't reserved for certain people. *Anyone* can be mentally tough! And I dare to say that it has nothing to do with appearing confident, either. Mental toughness is not about how you parade in front of others—it's about how you handle what life throws your way when you're all by yourself. It's not about appearances, but in having true confidence in your own ability to mentally process challenging events and issues.

Being mentally tough doesn't mean you'll never cry, complain, or be doubtful. Moreover, it does not preclude mental disease. In truth, a lot of people with ADHD, depression, and other mental health disorders are extraordinarily mentally strong individuals because they have to work so hard to create coping techniques.

Mental toughness examines the following issues rather than having a single, fixed definition of what it means to be mentally healthy: How do you handle distressing feelings or failures? Do you begin formulating ideas, complain about your misfortune, or simply let it roll off your back?

Defining Mental Toughness

Reframing negative thoughts and situations is a skill that requires both cognitive and emotional strength. Being mentally tough or strong enables us to fend against both internal and external forces that undermine our well-being and self-confidence.

Mental Toughness

To comprehend this concept, we can compare it to physical health. Mental strength is a part of mental fitness, just as physical strength is a part of physical fitness. In other words, the entire regimen of activities that enables you to maintain and enhance your mental state is known as mental fitness. At very crucial moments, this level of fitness can keep you focused. For instance, it can aid an athlete who needs to mentally silence the crowd to score the game-winning goal. Although mental toughness aids in performance under duress, it often is not long-lasting. This kind of severe strain can harm mental health even in Olympic competitors.

Yet, mental toughness strikes a balance between the extremes. It's our capacity to work productively and sustainably in the face of difficulties and stress, all while maintaining our overall health.

Psychological fitness includes: resilience, mental toughness, and mental strength. You can block out distractions and negative self-talk by having a strong mind. You can bounce back from setbacks with resilience. We can persevere with the aid of cognitive strength, while psychological fitness cultivates all of these skills.

Case Study

Jill is looking forward to making a presentation to her company's management soon. She practiced her slides, but her friend, Cathy, immediately identifies a flaw in her plan. Jill had worked diligently for weeks to get ready for this, so she is absolutely taken aback. Is there enough time for her to reassess her entire presentation? Probably not!

Luke Thybulle

Not all hope is lost; in fact, learning about the potential hazards may enable her to craft a more thorough presentation. She chooses to put into practice an activity that involves thinking of the worst-case scenario. But it takes mental toughness to adopt this problem-focused approach as opposed to panicking.

Jill decides to include another slide with her friend's concerns rather than scrapping the entire presentation or phoning in sick. She utilizes it as a springboard to invite questions and comments on the topic. Her diligence has pleased management, but they are also impressed by her sincerity and vision. She was able to overcome her fears and see the bright side as a result of her mental toughness.

- What would have happened if Jill wasn't mentally tough?

- Did Jill's friend do the right thing by pointing out the flaw?

- Was being taken aback a normal response to what happened?

- Have you ever been in a similar situation?

- How did you handle it?

- What would you do differently if the same situation arose?

Why It's Important to Be Mentally Tough

In many respects, mental toughness, along with an eye toward the future, is anxiety in action.

As you consider what anxiety is and why it exists, you realize that there is a reason for those unsettling feelings. Anxiety serves as a warning system to help us recognize potential dangers, and to help us prepare for them accordingly. Yet, it turns maladaptive when our fear paralyzes us.

We may fight off the effects of dread and anxiety and avoid becoming paralyzed by using our mental toughness. We are better equipped to reinterpret anxiety and understand what it is trying to teach us when we develop our mental strength. What possible consequences must we consider? What's the worst that might happen? And what can we do to increase our chances of success by preparing for it?

Mental toughness is a personality trait that represents your mindset. It analyzes your thoughts to determine why you behave in the way you do. So, there is a clear connection between mindset and behavior.

Some other significant effects of mental toughness on people are also evident. Here are five advantages of increasing mental toughness:

Discretion: Knowing what to listen to and what not to listen to is a necessary part of living a successful life. Internal and external criticism can both be quite confusing. Gaining mental toughness makes it far simpler to maintain your focus, even in the face of opposition or fear.

Luke Thybulle

The development of self-awareness and, consequently, emotional-management abilities depend on discretion. You'll grow more tolerant of your negative emotions as you learn to sit with them. You'll eventually discover which emotions are worthwhile addressing and which ones you should simply let go of.

If she dwelled on the issue that her friend found a flaw in her presentation, Jill would not have been able to think clearly and come up with an effective solution. What if she was so taken aback that she scrapped the entire presentation and tried to do it "better?"

She would have easily missed her deadline and come up short when it was time to present. Luckily, she used discretion and decided to turn the issue into a stepping stone by including it in her presentation. In the same way, when you receive criticism or have an uncomfortable thought, you can decide whether or not it will be useful.

Adaptability: Improving your ability to explore solutions makes you nimbler and more adaptable. You focus more on how you can get the desired result rather than obsessing over what isn't working correctly. You're also willing to consider the possibility that there may be more than one route, answer, or outcome that denotes success. You aren't afraid of change, so you don't get too dependent on having things happen precisely how you want them to.

Jill was definitely able to adapt. She took Cathy's advice, and instead of scrapping the presentation, she altered it. She was willing to acclimate to the situation and turn it into a strength.

Motivation: Our motivation and energy are sapped by poor mental strength. No matter what we try, it seems like horrible things always happen and nothing ever works in our favor. Conversely, those with a tough mental capacity have a high level of internal locus of control. This indicates that they believe they can change their situation. They are inspired to keep trying, developing, and seeking solutions by their sense of control. Those who are resilient don't give up easily.

Moreover, mental toughness provides the self-control and internal drive required to avoid procrastinating. Mentally tough individuals find it simpler to get going and finish projects.

Jill had enough motivation to work on the flaw of her presentation. She didn't ponder for too long. Instead, she immediately got to work and made an impressive presentation. If she lacked motivation, she could have easily hoped that management would overlook the flaw, or she could have just given up altogether.

Reduced Stress: When you have a strong mental foundation, the size of the circumstance doesn't stress you out as much. You regard difficulty as a chance to learn and develop. Even when significant events occur, you are able to reframe them and have faith in your ability to overcome them. After all, you've overcome significant challenges in the past, haven't you?

One of the best methods to enhance your general well-being is to manage your stress. Less stress is linked to a decreased risk of depression, anxiety, and various physical health issues.

Jill was bewildered, which is a natural response to criticism, especially if someone points out the truth. However, Jill was able to control the stress of the situation and use its energy to her advantage. What would've happened if she was overcome by stress and began panicking? She probably would have been fixated on the flaw and make a mess of everything. What are your thoughts?

Courage: You experience less fear of failing when you are mentally tough. Even when you are concerned about the outcome, it is still easier for you to enter the problem-solving mentality. You feel more confident about your abilities to identify solutions because you have higher levels of self-belief. You feel certain that you can endure the worst-case scenario, which is more vital (if it does come to pass).

When her friend pointed out the flaw, Jill was confident enough and had the courage to change her situation. Confidence and courage will help you in many stressful situations. As long as you believe in your abilities as Jill did, you can come up with effective solutions to difficult problems.

Those who are mentally tough produce more, work more purposefully, are more dedicated to their goals, and are more competitive. Better output, prompt and accurate delivery, as well as improved attendance result from this.

Additionally, strong-minded people exhibit greater attendance, are more likely to contribute to a positive culture, are more optimistic, have more "can do" qualities, adapt well to change and hardship, embrace responsibility, and are more inclined to volunteer for potential opportunities and activities.

For these reasons, having mental toughness is crucial for both an individual and an organization, especially during periods of significant change. Leaders, aspiring leaders, and anyone working in demanding, punishing jobs, or in unpredictable or rapidly changing environments need to adopt this mindset.

Everyday Habits for Building Mental Toughness

Finding habits and easy tricks to keep your energy up, your mindset positive, and to help you establish routines and skills that will help you move forward and keep you feeling positive about what you're doing are some of the best ways to build mental toughness. In the meantime, you're developing mental toughness with a technique that won't leave you feeling worn out and overloaded.

Here, you'll find habits you can cultivate to exercise your mental toughness.

The State of Your Bed Is the State of Your Head

Making your bed first thing in the morning is a terrific way to get things done and start the day off well. Although it can seem like a tiny step, it has significant advantages.

According to research, people who make their beds every day are generally happier with their life, more productive, and feel more pride and achievement for everything they accomplish throughout the day (Anderson, 2023). This seemingly small act, allows you to develop the habit of finishing tasks as soon as possible in the morning. Before you've even finished brushing your teeth, you've already completed one task!

Save Your Energy for What Matters

Get out there and be recognized. Take actions that make you happy. By forming healthy connections and letting go of unhealthy ones, you can strengthen your mental health.

It's often hard to let go of toxic people or environments, but you must resolve to become stronger. Throughout the day, you'll have more energy and happiness without the mental and emotional exhaustion.

Visualizing Your Goals

Spend some time (perhaps about 10 minutes each day) picturing your desired outcome as well as the difficulties you will face along the way. Try to carefully plan your route to accomplishing your goal in addition to picturing it. Develop your ability to visualize prospective difficulties and viable solutions. Imagine where you want to go and experience how wonderful it is to reach your goals.

By doing this you are toughening your mind and reprogramming it into believing that you can achieve any goal you set your mind to.

Decide to Eat Clean

There is a connection between gut health and mood, and one factor that directly affects gut health is the food you consume. You can lessen the strain on your digestive system by limiting foods that cause inflammation, such as any food allergens, cereals, dairy products, and alcohol. Less sick days and increased energy are benefits of a healthier digestive system, which can also lessen symptoms of stress and depression. Try to shop on the periphery of the grocery store and enjoy mainly homemade cuisine.

Do Something You Enjoy Doing Every Day

Look for a hobby or anything you enjoy doing merely for the sake of improving your mood.

As you become more proficient and confident in your chosen activity, you'll see how confidence and self-belief will spread to other aspects of your life. Your ability to think positively and enjoy your activity will help you become mentally stronger as you take on the more challenging parts of your goal.

Be Your Own Best Buddy

This is an excellent technique to develop mental toughness since it teaches us to rely on ourselves rather than constantly looking to others to boost our spirits. The next time something doesn't go as planned or you start to trash or criticize yourself, take a moment to think, "Would I allow my best friend to treat me this way?"

The likelihood is that you wouldn't, and loving yourself at least as much as your best buddy is a terrific thing.

Luke Thybulle

Record Your Gratitude

Write down something wonderful about each day, and store it somewhere safe—it can be a jar, a diary, a shoe box, or somewhere else. You will become more grateful as a result. Instead of only the challenges or difficult times that made you want to give up, you'll be able to reflect on the good things you've done and experienced at the end of the year.

You may be surprised at the amount of courage that accompanies a grateful heart. Maybe you'll still be afraid of some things, but being grateful will help you find the lessons to be learned in tough times, which means you'll be willing to do great things despite fear. And *that* is courage.

Journal in the Morning

Keep a journal and write at least three pages, or for five minutes, every morning or night. However, if you prefer to journal in the morning, you can express yourself creatively by writing about your dreams, and pouring all of your worries or concerns onto the page. It's also a terrific method to create an action plan, jot down your inspirations and goals for the day, and get a sense of what you want to accomplish.

If you decide to journal at night, unwind about anything that might have worried you, and acknowledge everything you accomplished.

Have Some Fun!

Anything fun will do; no matter how big or small. It may be something as simple as purchasing yourself your favorite bubble bath, seeing a movie, or buying a new outfit. It should be something you wouldn't ordinarily allow yourself to go for, something that will make you happy and make you feel good.

Allow yourself to indulge in a modest indulgence every month or few weeks, whether it's lighting a new candle or relaxing to new music you bought.

Be Inspired With Quotes

Encouragement can go a long way toward keeping you on track when times are difficult and you feel like you're not making any progress. Spend some time putting up some motivational sayings, images, or perhaps a vision board somewhere you'll see it every day.

When you're struggling, words of inspiration and motivation can help a great deal.

Sleep—It's Good for You

It's a big deal! You've seen young children go bonkers when they are exhausted, right? Adults react similarly, but we don't end up dozing off in the middle of our dinner plate. When you're overly exhausted, you make bad decisions, your mental strength declines, your rational mind becomes childlike, and your body reacts by producing more stress hormones.

Prioritize getting enough sleep to keep your mind sharp. If you're any kind of athlete, eight hours a day is a minimal requirement; the more, the better. If you're under stress, make sure you give yourself enough time to unwind and relax before bed so that your body can make the most of the sleeping hours.

Practice Daily Self-Care

Regardless of who you are or what you do, if you don't take the time to truly care for yourself, you'll soon run out of love and care to give to others.

Self-care can range from elaborate activities like getting a manicure or spending the day at a spa to basic actions like shutting oneself in the bathroom for five minutes to have some alone time. Whatever it is, make sure to create some space or activities that make you feel satisfied and content. It's hard for a drained mind to be tough!

Practice Mindful Happiness

Being present in the moment is the key to mindfulness. Practice being mindfully happy in order to get comfortable with being happy.

Choose a happy memory, experience, or moment and give yourself the freedom to indulge in it. See whether you can tie any colors to your emotions by observing how it rests in your body, how your thoughts and body change, and how it feels.

Spend some time in a joyful frame of mind. In the end, pay attention to the sensation of joy and contentment that arises naturally when you are mindful in the moment.

Be Your Own Cheerleader

Holding on to negative thoughts can ruin your mindset and weaken your mind. How can you have mental toughness if you only believe bad things about yourself?

Commit to increasing your positive thoughts and rejecting negative thoughts that enter your mind. Consider how amazing you'll feel as you make better and stronger decisions about your life. It may feel silly at first, but this will keep you moving in the direction of your objective.

Be aware that negative thoughts can enter your head very fast; when you catch them, simply acknowledge that they are false (even if you have to do it aloud) and replace them with positive thoughts.

Luke Thybulle

Remove "Should" From Your Vocabulary

When was the last time you felt you should have done something? Not exactly a delightful or interesting thought, was it?

Rarely does the word "should" elicit thoughts of joy but more of obligation and weighty responsibility. "Should" often connotes harsh judgment and self-criticism, neither of which contributes to the foundation you're setting to strengthen your mind.

Change the word "should" to anything you are looking forward to doing. "I would like to be mentally stronger," as an example, or "I want to get healthier physically."

Stop Living to Please People

We often overextend ourselves and commit to things we really don't want to undertake in an effort to be good people.

Recognize that you can never please everyone. Give up the desire to put other people's goals and happiness before your own.

Cut Down on Social Media Time

On social media, we often put our best foot forward, which can lead to us trying to compare our lives to the highlights reel of someone else's life. You can feel lousy and unsatisfied with your life's circumstances, forgetting all the wonderful things you've achieved. You can also lose sight of the many wonderful lives that you inspire every day just by being the extraordinary person that you are.

Cut your time on social media by half, and start socializing with loved ones, reading a book, or engaging in a pastime you find enjoyable. Make sure that whatever you choose to do will boost your spirits.

More "Thank You's" and Less Complaining

A cycle of complaining can make you difficult to be around, but it can also be very detrimental to your mental health. Try to find something to be grateful for rather than just whining nonstop about a difficult situation.

Learn to Say "No" Without Feeling Guilty

We as a society have come to the view that merely not wanting to do something is not a sufficient justification for saying no. Chuck it out if you catch yourself thinking along that line.

Say "no" more often. No one should require you to justify your choices or give an explanation for why you decline doing something.

Find the Positivity in Every Challenge

Perspective plays a big part in life. You may transform your life by altering your perspective.

Build up your positive mental strength by noting the positive aspects and lessons you could be learning from any problems that may arise, rather than complaining, getting angry or disappointed, or engaging in negative conversations about them. Make an effort to find something to be thankful for each day.

Times can be tough, and that's the main reason we need to be mentally tough. We should be able to rely on ourselves and our own strengths. I'm not saying that we must cut other people out altogether, but how often do you find yourself in a challenging situation with no one around to uplift or support you? Or, people may be close but have no idea *how* to support you.

Mental resilience walks hand-in-hand with mental toughness. In the next chapter, we'll talk about mental resilience, how it affects mental toughness and vice versa, and habits you can develop to build mental resilience.

Chapter 2: Understanding Mental Resilience

When translated, the Latin phrase *"Mens sana in corpore sano"*, means "a healthy mind in a healthy body." We should be more conscious than ever of how intertwined these two elements are, especially in the modern world. Our mental and physical health are seriously threatened by any type of stress or catastrophe. We can maintain our balance when we have a healthy level of resilience.

The ability to be resilient allows us to handle the stress and keep a good, positive attitude throughout these difficult times, ensuring that we don't lose our footing.

Our level of resilience is influenced by a variety of factors. We'll go through the most crucial traits and abilities for resilience and inner strength in this chapter. To become more resilient, we must first learn how to overcome obstacles and deal with stress. Only then, can we concentrate on developing and honing these abilities to become more mentally resilient.

Understanding the Concept of Resilience

One way to think of resilience is as the immune system of the mind and psyche. While some people possess a high level of emotional resilience by nature, others must first learn and hone this skill.

Luke Thybulle

Those that are resilient are thought to be optimistic, solution-focused, flexible, and innovative. They are able to bounce speedily from setbacks, manage stress and difficulties, and seize opportunities when they arise. Always thinking of possibilities and how to effectively solve problems are some characteristics of those with strong resilience.

Resilience, often referred to as adaptability, is the process by which individuals respond to issues and changes in their environment by changing their behavior. This procedure entails:

- triggers that call for resilience (such as trauma or distress)

- resources to help you be resilient (like self-confidence, a supportive social environment, and a positive attitude toward life)

- consequences (for example, changes in behavior or attitudes)

Being resilient can significantly improve a person's capacity to bounce back from setbacks or adapt to change.

Simply put, individuals who possess the psychological and behavioral skills necessary to remain composed in the face of turmoil or crises, and to recover from the occurrence without suffering long-term negative effects, are said to have mental resilience.

So, is mental resilience the same as mental health? Our social, emotional, and psychological well-being are all aspects of mental health. According to Mind, every year roughly one out of four persons suffer mental health issues (Rosie, 2014). I advise anyone experiencing persistent mental health issues to consult a doctor as soon as you can. Interventions for workplace mental resilience are not advised for those who are off the job due to or have recently returned from concerns with their mental health.

Developing your mental resilience is something we can view as preparation for life's disappointments. Consider this: Your chances of staying dry are substantially higher if you put your raincoat on before you venture outside. But it's also important to realize that some days it will rain, and that's alright.

Some people are born with an inclination to be buoyant, while others are not. And that's normal because we are all born different. Every one of us has a unique genetic makeup. These variations affect each person's capacity to respond physiologically to stressful conditions. So, the various internal mechanisms that control how we respond to various events are there from birth. This does not, however, represent the entire picture.

As we are more likely to encounter certain circumstances as adults, we have probably developed several coping mechanisms without even realizing it. Most of the resources we need to develop resilience are available to us through training and experience (experiential learning). But there are occasions when you need someone else to help you reach your full potential, much like how a personal trainer may help gym attendees or leadership teams in the workplace.

You must be careful, though. It is possible to become *too* mentally resilient. You need to establish the perfect balance, just like with most things in life. Although it's rare, there are potential dangers to be aware of if you do become overly resilient:

- You start saying "yes" a lot. Then, you end up becoming the "go-to" person for every tedious or challenging duty, which can make you feel bitter.

- You become the rock for everyone else. This position requires a great deal of effort. Also, you won't have much time to convey or process your own feelings.

Lack of mental resilience can manifest itself in different ways in the workplace. Every person is built differently, as we just established. The employee's skill set should become more balanced as a result of learning resilience, and situational stress should be decreased.

Employees should receive training to assist them in learning effective coping mechanisms. If properly conducted, this training ought to enhance employees' productivity as well as their mental health.

Mental resilience is not only important in the workplace. You can use every coping mechanism for enhancing strength in your regular day-to-day activities as well. In fact, experiential learning is one of the fundamental principles of mental resilience.

You'll encounter unfamiliar situations, both at home and in the office. You will gain coping mechanisms from each experience. These experiences will teach you some new coping mechanisms that you can use in similar situations in the future.

Don't feel ashamed if you realize that you lack mental toughness or resilience. Perhaps, you have faced more challenging situations than most, who knows? The good news is that regardless of your experiences, you *can* learn to be mentally tough and resilient.

How Mental Resilience Is Related to Mental Toughness

First of all, mental toughness and mental resilience are not the same concept. There is a distinction and, although the two principles are similar, there are substantial differences.

However, the terms are now frequently used interchangeably, which could mean that the intended result is targeted but not realized. The ability to bounce back from adversity is referred to as resilience. This implies that those who are resilient can deal with adversity when it occurs.

The meaning of "resilience" has shifted, and there are now numerous variations on the original definitions that seem to widen it. This adds a confusing component that sidesteps the problem. For instance, we frequently observe that the concepts of mental toughness and mental resilience are becoming more congruent.

Luke Thybulle

When we talk about mental toughness, some people could respond by saying, "That's what I mean by resilience." But then it is no longer a description of resilience—they are describing mental toughness.

Because the original definitions highlight a significant point, it is helpful to go back to them. A person is referred to as resilient if they are able to deal with adversity. Being able to handle a challenge or setback well is a helpful, valuable, and desirable skill. But it doesn't necessarily imply that they felt positive about their experience. They might have simply clenched their jaws and carried on because "it needed to be done."

Without other factors (such as a positive attitude), excessive exposure to hardship and adversity can and frequently wear one down. Resilience can be viewed as a passive or neutral property in its most basic form. "I am a resilient person because I must be. rather than...because I want to be."

People have different responses to pressure, opportunity, and challenges. Even if everyone may aspire to be resilient, some people choose to view difficulties and obstacles positively, perhaps even seeking them out. Because of their propensity for exposure to risk, challenge, and opportunity, these people typically handle disappointments better (as well as repeated setbacks). This concept is of mental toughness and is separate from the notion of resilience.

There is a difference between wanting resilience because it is necessary and wanting it because it is an admirable trait you wish to have.

Let's add the idea of positivity to the scene. Some people may view a problem or difficulty as a challenge and be more solution-focused than others; seeing opportunity where others would see a threat.

Some of this has been incorporated into the concept of mental toughness's challenging component. This kind of strength consists of confidence and can be described as a personality characteristic that, regardless of the situation, greatly influences how an individual will mentally react to pressure, opportunity, and challenge. A psychologically tough individual sees struggle and adversity as an opportunity and not a threat and has the confidence and positive outlook to accept what appears on their path.

Hence, mental toughness and mental resilience are connected. Most, if not all, mentally tough people are mentally resilient, but not all mentally resilient people are mentally tough. The positive element makes the difference.

A mentally resilient individual can bounce back from a bad event either partially or entirely. That does not necessarily indicate that the individual feels positive about the negative circumstance.

> *Something went wrong, but I'm going to persevere and get back up, and I still feel that I can do some or all of what I initially intended, despite this setback. I'm going to try my best to accomplish some or all of my goals.*

These are the kinds of thoughts that a resilient person usually thinks. Although having an optimistic or positive outlook would be helpful, resilience does not require this condition.

Therefore, a person who lacks optimism and confidence can still be resilient but may still find things difficult. They may also be more prone to wilt if they are required to be resilient too often or for too long.

Is it essential to differentiate between toughness and resilience? I believe so.

Experiential learning can help people increase both their resilience and mental toughness. This can be achieved either through intentional development, coaching, or just going through the motions of life.

In a world where everyone encounters change, difficulties, and setbacks more often and faster than ever before, the result is slightly different but nonetheless significant. Positivity is vital; it involves being "comfortable in your own skin" and accepting the ups and downs of life as a journey. It is a step in the process of developing oneself.

When comparing the two, it may be helpful to apply the concept of "survive and thrive." You can survive by having mental resilience and thrive by being mentally tough.

It matters because the result is more positive and leads to:

- improved efficiency
- improved and sustained well-being
- cultivation of constructive habits
- increased ambitions

These are significant outcomes for organizations and people, either separately or collectively.

The Pillars of Mental Resilience

Our level of resilience is influenced by seven key aspects (Schuy, 2022). The model, commonly referred to as the "seven pillars of resilience," highlights the key abilities and components of inner fortitude and perseverance.

Pillar One: An Effective Personal Network

This pillar focuses on creating and developing a reliable, close-knit support system. Your partner, friends, family, and others from your social and professional circles could make up the network. At times of need or disaster, you can reach out to your personal network for support, which will help you overcome obstacles and setbacks.

Where your capabilities run out is where strong relationships kick in. When there is a group of people that share similar values, it creates a system of giving, receiving, and sharing. The people in your network should ideally have a wide range of skills that they can draw on in difficult situations.

Being among others naturally boosts confidence and helps people become more resilient to stress, problems, and potential crises.

Pillar Two: Be Focused on Solutions

Instead of focusing on problems, resilient people consider opportunities and solutions. You will inevitably face a variety of difficulties and crises during your life that keeps you up at night. Those who are resilient handle these circumstances better and are more likely to develop workable solutions.

Pillar Three: Acceptance—Knowing How to Let Go

Stress is reduced and making decisions is made simpler by accepting and letting go. Several factors that have an impact on your life are beyond your control. But you have a lot of control over the way you perceive things and respond to them.

This acceptance is frequently hampered by perfectionism. Most perfectionists are completely unaware of this reality, which is unfortunate. They are experts at self-criticism, and continuously feel the need to perform flawlessly, as well as take full responsibility for anything that doesn't go according to plan, regardless if they were truly at fault or not.

Pillar Four: Shape Your Future

Mentally resilient people are aware that they're able to shape their future. They actively pursue their objectives and a fulfilling life by making a conscious effort to achieve these goals.

Setting the correct goals and keeping a healthy work-life balance are all important aspects of planning for the future, as are eating well and taking care of your physical needs.

Pillar Five: Overcoming the Victim Mentality

It's time to move outside our comfort zone and begin accepting responsibility for our lives rather than being inactive and feeling helpless.

We must put an end to complaining and directing blame, and accept ownership of our thoughts, feelings, words, and deeds. When things get difficult, we should make an effort to maintain our composure and confidence by using the power of intention and living in the present.

Practicing self-reflection and challenging and altering our attitudes and belief systems are two ways to do this. It is also easier for us to accept responsibility for our actions when we have a positive view of ourselves and high self-confidence.

Pillar Six: Dare to Be Optimistic

Those that are optimistic always attempt to find the positive aspects of a situation. This optimistic outlook frequently generates fresh concepts, useful solutions, and successful results. Optimists are certain that crises and difficulties will pass relatively quickly and be overcome. However, being optimistic does not entail being delusional or deaf to reality.

Positive and negative possibilities and viewpoints should always be in healthy proportion. One doesn't reject the reality of negative things by focusing on the positive aspects and dedicating one's attention to solving a problem.

For the optimist, the glass is half full, but for the pessimist, it is half empty. Which one are you?

Pillar Seven: Introspection

Self-reflection and introspection are essential components of resilience. Part of being attentive to your thoughts, actions, and emotions lies in finding the answers to the following question:

- Who is the real me?

- How do I want others to see me?

- How does my mindset affect my thoughts, feelings, and behaviors?

- What are my strengths, abilities, personality traits, needs, and desires?

- How do I want to live and work, and how can I achieve that?

Self-reflection is a skill that can be acquired with some consistent practice. It is the art of sincerely and thoroughly examining your thoughts, feelings, and behavior, coming to the appropriate conclusions, and accepting accountability.

Everyday Habits for Building Mental Resilience

It requires a lot of practice to increase your emotional resilience. This is because mental fortitude—the capacity to overcome hardship—isn't always innate. How we respond to adversity depends on the circumstances. We can develop poor habits that sap our energy and strength over time. Thankfully, we can change some of these unhealthy habits. Let's explore seven resilience-enhancing techniques you can employ every day to become a stronger, happier version of yourself.

Establish a Healthy Morning Routine

Our capacity for mental resilience is weakened by a lack of control and indecisiveness. Establish a morning routine to handle both of these at once. It eliminates indecision and inactivity at the beginning of your day. In this sense, it puts you in the driver's seat of your day from the time you wake up.

Each person has a unique morning ritual. For instance, the morning rituals of successful entrepreneurs vary greatly. Exercise energizes the body and improves physical toughness and resilience. On the other hand, responding to emails and creating a task list assist you in organizing the remaining hours of your day. Regardless of what you decide, the structure and sense of accomplishment will give you the drive to face the rest of the day head-on.

End the Day with a Healthy Evening Routine

Creating an evening routine gives your day more structure, just like your morning routine does. It offers a method for winding down. You could start by attending to the minor details that cause you to feel sluggish in the morning. For example, make the coffee or lay out the clothing for the following day. These quick routines not only assist in getting your day started but also mark the end of the workday. Your evening routine can now start.

Reading, journaling, or meditation are all excellent nighttime rituals. Each one enables you to let go of the tension and worry you brought with you. They also help your mind become more open to letting go of bothersome thoughts that can keep you up at night. These methods of stress relief enhance emotional resilience by promoting calmness and relaxation. In addition, they get your body and mind ready for a deeper, more restorative sleep.

Practice Gratitude

Our minds can spiral into self-defeating notions of inadequacy when we worry. Spend some time each day reminding yourself of what you have to be grateful for. You might reflect on your own special talents or abilities that helped you get through difficult times. Just think of all the external things you have to be thankful for. They might include close friends, pets, or even particular possessions that improve your quality of life. You might even think about keeping a gratitude journal. Whatever method you choose, this daily practice of gratitude can help you overcome adversity and strengthen your mental resilience.

Welcome New Challenges

This one might initially seem illogical. How does taking on more challenges increase resilience, given that more challenges increase stress which ultimately harms resilience? But when we are not engaging in activities, we typically worry the most. Taking on an interesting new challenge instantly refocuses the mind. In other words, it focuses your efforts on a problem you can immediately fix.

Sometimes, the solution is as straightforward as confronting your own biases. Are you likely to decline a new dish or an after-work gathering? Instead, say "yes". Almost every day presents a special chance to try something new. These modest successes will increase your self-confidence and sense of accomplishment. Other times, it will solidify your biases so that you can say "no" with confidence when necessary.

Visualize

Your mind and body suffer as a result of ongoing stress and anxiety. While fear typically lasts only a short while, worry might persist for days or even weeks. Your body is directly and negatively affected by such anxiety. In actuality, it causes the same chemicals to be released as when we are in danger. Such protracted stress causes fatigue, irritation, and loss of focus. In other words, a decline in physical, mental, and emotional resilience.

Visualization exercises assist us in facing our fears head-on. These might be anything from picturing yourself succeeding in a challenging situation to envisioning your preferred serene environment. Practicing this during your daily commute, before lunch, or before you go to bed will help release some pent-up stress.

Soak Up the Sun

When you spend time outside, do you feel better? That isn't only your imagination. Our physical and mental health can improve through the use of ecotherapy. It revitalizes us and aids in our ability to recover. In other words, it increases our emotional and physical resilience. We grow more resilient and content.

A mountain hideaway or a woodland trail is not mandatory, either. Simply set out some time each day to go outside and enjoy the sun and environment. There could be a patio at your place of business. You may perhaps go for a stroll through the neighborhood after work or at lunch. Even in an urban setting, there is a wealth of sky, sun, grass, and trees. Use them to your advantage. If your workplace is very stressful, taking a walk in the nearby neighborhood around lunchtime can help you recharge. Your determination will be strengthened while being renewed by this daily activity.

Use Productive Talk

The words we use to speak to ourselves and others greatly influence how we perceive ourselves. Negative words have the ability to emotionally and physically drain us. Exercises that improve the words we speak strengthen our mental and emotional resilience.

What about the way we communicate with others, though?

Do you recall Jill from Chapter 1? Think about the following circumstance. Jill had two options on how to respond when her friend pointed out the flaw in her presentation:

- "Thanks; I'll take care of the problem and update the presentation. I don't understand why I always do stupid things like that!"

- "I appreciate you bringing that to my attention! I'll take care of the problem and update the presentation."

Not only does Jill accept the input in the first instance, but you can also see that she is doubting herself. She even bolsters such doubt by asserting that she "always" makes such "stupid" errors. The second response, though, is all positive. She sounds secure in her ability to handle the situation as she transitions from self-doubt to appreciation.

Be aware of the times when your language feeds your self-doubts. Added to unfavorable words used, even small amounts of negativity might eventually make us less positive and harm our resilience.

What we've seen in this chapter is that mental toughness is the ability to handle a challenging situation without panic, while mental resilience helps a person to persevere despite lingering hardships.

We can build our resilience with the help of personal networks, knowing when to let go, and planning our futures. Thereafter, there are habits we can develop to further increase our resilience, such as practicing gratitude, using visualizations, and developing healthy morning and evening routines.

However, if you have a fixed mindset, try as you might, you may have great difficulty cultivating mental toughness. That is why we'll discuss how you can overcome limiting beliefs and adopt a growth mindset in the next chapter.

Chapter 3: Stop Limiting Yourself and Start Growing!

The stories we tell ourselves about our identities that prevent us from becoming the people we were meant to be are known as limiting beliefs. These beliefs prevent us from reaching our full potential. They are usually subconscious, and until someone points them out to us, we aren't even aware that we have them.

The brain is programmed to save energy. We desire certainty in our habits, relationships, and careers. We often avoid risk and prefer to stay in our comfort zones, meaning that we only put effort into action when we think doing so will result in success. We give up before we even begin when we don't have a strong sense of self-belief or when we don't think we can accomplish our goals. We don't give it all we've got and undermine our own success. That sums up limiting beliefs in its most basic form. It doesn't sound like mental toughness at all, does it?

Limiting beliefs are often associated with a fixed mindset. When you have a fixed mindset, your current abilities take precedence over your potential for the future. Individuals with this mentality typically avoid difficulties out of fear of failing since they are unaware that their effort will influence their future. They rely on feedback from others to determine whether their job is satisfactory.

Your life could be negatively impacted by a fixed mindset, resulting in your inability to learn or develop. It is a mentality that restricts your future potential and keeps you from attaining your objectives. When times are rough, it discourages you and prevents you from trying new things. Also, it restricts your growth, mental toughness, and commitment.

If you're struggling with achieving success or realize that you're holding yourself back, don't despair. You're not alone in this, and together we'll work on correcting our beliefs and conquering a fixed mindset.

So, let's explore limiting beliefs and how to overcome them, as well as how you can step out of your comfort zone and cultivate a growth mindset, as this is essential to establishing and maintaining mental toughness.

Understanding Limiting Beliefs

Although every one of us has limitless potential, our results often don't match that. Why? Because our results are hampered by our unconscious beliefs. Limiting beliefs have an impact on every aspect of our life and can impede us in many different ways. By nature, we only put effort into things we think will lead to the results we want. Consequently, when we take half-hearted action because we think things won't work out, even unknowingly, we destroy our potential. Inaction leads to poor results. Poor results equate to doubt and discouraged beliefs. It is a vicious loop that can only be broken when you decide to alter your input.

The loop is called *the success cycle* (Robbins, 2015) and works like this:

$$\begin{array}{ccc} \textbf{Potential} & \rightarrow & \textbf{Action} \\ \uparrow & & \downarrow \\ \textbf{Beliefs} & \leftarrow & \textbf{Results} \end{array}$$

In other words:

- When we realize we have potential, it leads to action.

- After we have taken action, it leads to results.

- The results are witnessed by ourselves and affect our beliefs about ourselves.

- What we believe about ourselves affects what we believe is our potential, which again leads to action.

Each of these terms stands on its own and is generally self-explanatory, but when combined to form the success cycle, we gain a deeper understanding of the psychology of success.

The success formula is depicted in the diagram above. We will be able to achieve greater potential if our beliefs about attaining something are stronger. More potential leads to increased action. Better actions provide more effective results.

However, if we don't take care, the success cycle also can operate in reverse. Beliefs have the ability to both create and destroy.

Luke Thybulle

So, what exactly is a belief? It's a sense of assurance regarding the meaning of something. The problem is that most of our beliefs were subconsciously formed depending on how we chose to interpret both positive and negative prior experiences. Nevertheless, unless you want to stay there, the past does not control the present. Almost every belief can be supported by experiences, but the trick is to make sure that we are aware of the beliefs we are developing. Change your beliefs if they do not empower you.

Will you refrain from taking the necessary actions to achieve the outcomes you want in life because of your beliefs? Or are you going to turn them into the ideal chance to create something exceptional, whether it be a change in yourself, your family, or your career? The story you repeatedly tell yourself is quite possibly the only thing preventing you from achieving your goals.

Examples of Limiting Beliefs

Here are some examples of limiting beliefs. Can you identify with any of them?

I'm Not Capable

It's easy to tell ourselves this when it comes to our careers. It frequently hides a fear of failure or, occasionally, a fear of triumph. We think, "I couldn't accomplish that," particularly when we contrast ourselves with others. "I lack the necessary abilities." But what's this? Any skill can be learned with determination and faith.

I'm Not Deserving of Love

This is one of the most prevalent limiting notions in relationships. When we feel unworthy of love, we may reject every potential mate, ruin our relationships via quarreling and infidelity, or refrain from dating at all. This is not a way to live.

I Don't Have the Time

Almost everyone on the planet has used this excuse. But, when something is important to you—work, goal, or relationship—you find time for it. The day is the same length for everyone. What you do with it is what counts.

I Am Not Strong Enough

This belief holds us in our comfort zone. We don't believe we have the mental toughness to overcome rejection, failure, or discomfort. To avoid possible hurt, we prefer to remain where we are.

We all have limitless potential, and that's the reality. The road to success begins with this belief. We can realize our full potential if we truly think that we are competent and worthy of achievement. This encourages more action, which in turn encourages better outcomes. This strengthens our self-confidence, and the cycle repeats itself with even more power. This cycle of achievement is accessible to everyone. Identifying your limiting beliefs is the first step.

How recently have you given up on something, and why? When did you last fail, and what did you tell yourself about why you failed? Any other self-talk than "I did my best, I learned a lesson, and I will do better next time", is an excuse. You're allowing limiting beliefs to prevent you from accomplishing your objectives.

Techniques for Overcoming Limiting Beliefs

It's not always easy to get rid of limiting beliefs. We have them firmly ingrained in us, typically since childhood. But you may learn how to get rid of your limiting beliefs once you realize what they are and how to recognize them. You can finally realize all of your goals by integrating practical techniques for overcoming limiting beliefs into your daily life.

Let's talk about techniques you can use as tools to overcome limiting beliefs.

Accept Responsibility

Many people rarely accept responsibility for their lives, which is the main cause of their failure to achieve their goals. Some people choose to think that things simply happen to them and for that reason, they don't need to be responsible. This is referred to as an external locus of control, and is a limiting belief in and of itself. You need to establish an internal locus of control, or the belief that life happens for you, not to you, in order to learn how to overcome your limiting beliefs. While what happens to us is out of our control, we choose how to respond, which means our fate is ultimately decided by our actions.

Regardless, we can control our emotions, learn from mistakes, make better judgments, and move toward our objectives.

Pay Attention to Your Inner Voice

We have touched on this issue in Chapter 1, but it is also a key component of overcoming limiting beliefs. Your limiting beliefs may sometimes reside in the depths of your subconscious, but more often than not, it is your inner critic who is telling you why you are unable, unwilling, or should refrain from doing something. You constantly hear your inner voice, and the more you listen to it, the more you start to believe it.

Humans have thousands of thoughts per day—possibly even tens of thousands—and if even a small percentage of them are limiting beliefs, that creates a persistently negative image in your mind.

The first step in overcoming limiting beliefs is to become aware of how your inner voice speaks to you. What does it say when you fail or give up on a task? Does getting ready for a date or a night out with friends make you feel upbeat or nervous? Put down any negative thoughts, and then observe which ones recur. They are your limiting beliefs. Make an effort to recognize these thoughts, stop them, and replace them with more empowering ones.

Leave Certainty Behind

This may sound like madness. Why leave certainty behind? Isn't it a good quality? It often is anything other than good. Why is it so difficult to get rid of limiting beliefs? We all seek certainty as it provides us with comfort and security in our lives when used sparingly. Yet, certainty can sometimes be a hindrance. You can't leave the job you despise because of it. It's what keeps you in unhealthily close friendships and familial interactions as well as romantic partnerships. That's why you decided against writing a book or taking that trip to Greece.

Limiting beliefs are certainty's closest friend, and both kill dreams. Dream big rather than dwelling on what you'll never accomplish. Take the rocking chair test to determine what you would regret most when you are old and gray and reflect on your life. It is an effective motivator for getting rid of limiting beliefs.

Determine Your Limiting Beliefs

Our limiting beliefs are notions we have about the world and ourselves that keep us from reaching our full potential. They hinder us in several ways, giving us the impression that we're unworthy of success, that we're not as good as others, and that everyone is out to get us. Typically, they fall into four categories:

Other People

Obsessing over what others think of you means having limiting beliefs about other people. The limiting thought that underlies social anxiety is often, "Others will think I'm X." Replace X to complete the sentence with thoughts that run through your mind, such as awkward, foolish, or unlovable. This kind of limiting belief, which holds that others will be disappointed or won't love you if you don't act in a particular way, is where the need for perfection emerges.

While we have social norms to adhere to, obsessing about the opinions of others is never healthy and can cause a dent to your mental toughness. Empower yourself and cultivate your inner strength by making a decision, and sticking to it, so that you will stop worrying about what other people think of you. Learn to love yourself. Become your own best friend. Change the way you think about yourself. If a limiting thought or belief comes knocking, send it away. If you're worried that someone may not like you, think about it this way: It will be *their* loss! The fact that you *want* to cultivate mental toughness says a lot about you—you desire change and a better future. That makes you a phenomenal person already.

Entitled Beliefs

What if I told you that sometimes having limiting beliefs can feel empowering? Many times, arguments for avoiding change and staying in your comfort zone include thinking that the world owes you something, that you're superior to others, or that people just "don't get" you.

Luke Thybulle

Understand that no one owes you anything. The success you crave—you have to work for. The relationship you want—you have to do what is necessary to make it bloom. The career you want—you have to learn and grow and be willing to be uncomfortable at times, well away from your comfort zone. The point is, everything you want that is good, is your responsibility. No one else.

It Is What It Is

These are preconceived notions about "how things are," including the belief that you have no influence over your circumstances. One common limitation is a lack of time. Denial is another limiting worldview, such as the belief that true love doesn't exist or that it is tough to find jobs that are fulfilling. One of the most difficult things we can accomplish in life is to change our negative self-talk, yet once we do, we are rewarded with unimaginable possibilities.

Step out and go see the world. Find things that contradict your limiting beliefs. There *are* people who have fulfilling careers. There *is* enough time to make a difference. There *are* people who have found true love and are in healthy and fulfilling relationships. If others can have it, so can you.

What You Believe About Yourself

Limiting beliefs about yourself arise when you believe that you are innately awkward, foolish, or unlovable, as opposed to caring what others think. Other prevalent self-beliefs include the notions that you are too young, too ugly, or incapable of learning new skills. None of these statements are true. These are merely the stories you tell yourself—stories that you're free to change. You have the power over your own story!

A Growth Mindset

Everyone has inherent skills that, when developed with a growth mindset, can be enhanced. Writing, mathematics, creativity, and fact memorization are a few of these skills. Nobody is born with impeccable talents, though. You can maximize your potential and accomplish your goals by adopting a growth mindset. An individual with a growth mindset doesn't take themselves too seriously and is never scared to make mistakes. Acquiring a new skill requires effort and repetition.

The term "growth mindset" was coined by Carol Dweck, a professor of psychology at Stanford University. She did a lot of research on the effects of the mindset when it comes to developing skills and learning (Dutton, 2015).

People with a fixed mindset usually avoid difficulties out of fear of failing. They might attempt to escape their responsibilities in such a circumstance. Those who are growth-minded view challenges as exciting opportunities because they recognize they'll gain new insights from them. They persist in tough circumstances, learn to control them, and eventually advance to even bigger achievements.

A growth mindset has several advantages and learning from mistakes is more likely to occur in those who have a growth mindset. For instance, Jill made an effort to improve her presentation when her friend pointed out the flaw in it. While working on new projects, Jill started to appreciate taking on new difficulties, as she has accepted that there's still a lot to learn.

Owning your own development is one strategy to promote a growth mindset. Reflect on your accomplishments and shortcomings and add those words to your vocabulary. In a similar vein, if you're a teacher, make sure to mention your flaws in your students' assessments. You need to take better care of yourself than you might believe. Self-care enhances both a person's personal and professional lives.

Everyday Habits for Building a Growth Mindset

The belief that talents and abilities can be developed and that making a conscious effort to develop and expand them would strengthen them as a result is defined as a growth mindset. A fixed mindset, on the other hand, is the conviction that, despite our best efforts, our skills are unchangeable and fixed.

You can have a fixed mindset in some areas of life and a growth mindset in others. Try establishing these habits, and if you can, identify a fixed mindset in your life and want to change it to one of growth:

Failures Don't Define You

Learn to see failure as a temporary setback rather than as something that completely defines you. This will help to avoid falling into the fixed mindset trap. Even though they still encounter failure and disappointment, people who have a growth mindset don't let these setbacks stop them from achieving their objectives. When things don't go according to plan, adopt a growth mindset and concentrate on what you can do differently thereafter.

Your Words Have Power

Consider the effect your words have on the people around you. Do you encourage others to learn, grow, and develop in your relationships by adopting a growth mindset? If not, spend some time considering how you can enhance your relationships with people at work and at home to promote a growth mindset culture.

Don't Let Negativity Stop You

Be careful not to let harmful criticism sidetrack or demotivate you when you resolve to overcome bad habits. While constructive criticism can be beneficial, it's equally crucial to cultivate and pay attention to your own inner, growth-minded voice. Determine whether the criticism you get, both from yourself and others, stems from a fixed mindset or from a growth mindset. When coaching oneself, think about how you would encourage a friend or coworker who was starting a new learning experience.

Be Receptive to New Knowledge and Experiences

A fixed mindset effectively switches people off to learning. A growth mentality, on the other hand, keeps brain activity continuously high and results in greater learning than a fixed mindset. Being open to new experiences and knowledge is crucial because when we do, our neurons fire and connect, helping us to expand our talents and abilities with a growth mindset.

Celebrate Your Achievements

Your drive to attempt new things, persist, and reach your potential is directly influenced by your confidence in your skills. Spend some time celebrating and acknowledging your accomplishments. Recognize the effort that has helped you master a new skill or achieve success in a current area of interest. Remember past successes that required learning, and remind yourself that having a growth mindset helped you succeed, as you start a new learning curve.

Visualize a Successful Outcome

A key element of success is the ability to concentrate on the satisfying emotions you will feel once you have achieved your objective. Create a mental picture of what success would look like. Maintain a sharp focus on your intended result and visualize how amazing you will feel once you have mastered your new subject or ability.

Zealously Take on New Challenges

Don't shy away from challenges you've previously felt unable to overcome. It is possible to learn new skills and talents by tackling challenging activities. Roads are comparable to the synaptic connections that form during learning in the brain. The most heavily traveled roads are widened. The ones that aren't utilized very often deteriorate. The opportunity to learn new skills and make new synaptic connections presented by challenging or new tasks can increase your performance over time.

It is imperative to overcome limiting beliefs and escape a fixed mindset. Only then can you truly cultivate mental toughness as you will believe that you can take on anything. With positive beliefs and a growth mindset, you'll understand that there isn't truly such a thing as failing, as with every setback comes a valuable lesson. And if you choose so, these lessons can only make you smarter and mentally tougher.

For a growth mindset to properly function, you will need a lot of positive thinking. We'll talk about having a positive mindset and how to overcome negativity in the next chapter.

Luke Thybulle

Chapter 4: Building a Positive Mindset

You probably don't find it surprising that positivity is fundamental to positive psychology. But, being positive is more than just laughing and being upbeat; it also refers to one's outlook on life as a whole and their propensity to highlight everything in a favorable way.

The foundations of positive psychology will be covered in this chapter, along with some of the many advantages of adopting a positive outlook on life. We'll also look at some practical advice and methods for developing a positive mindset.

This kind of mindset consists of a propensity to see the good in things, to hope for the best, and to take on problems with positivity. Making the most of any circumstance you find yourself in and developing the practice of productive thinking.

The Effects of Positive Thinking

What does it look like when someone has a positive mindset? There are many different characteristics, but here are some examples:

- **Mindfulness:** Focusing the mind on conscious awareness and improving attention span.

- **Resilience:** Rebounding back from hardship, disappointment, and failure instead of giving up.

- **Integrity:** The quality of being honest, upright, and forthright rather than dishonest and self-serving.

- **Acceptance:** Realizing that things don't always go as planned, but also taking responsibility for your actions and learning from them.

- **Gratitude:** The practice of actively and consistently acknowledging your blessings.

- **Optimism:** A readiness to make an effort and take risks instead of assuming your hard work won't pay off.

These traits are not only indicative of a positive mindset, but they must also be exercised willingly and consciously. By intentionally incorporating optimism, acceptance, resilience, appreciation, mindfulness, and integrity into your life, you may cultivate and sustain a positive mindset.

Let's look at similar qualities. Can you relate to any of the following?

When you have a positive mindset, you are able to face challenges without panicking. When you don't receive something that you've wanted, you don't throw a fit. Also, when something unexpected happens—even if it is something you didn't want to happen—you still feel good about it. You constantly motivate people around you with your positivity. You are like a source of energy that inspires and empowers others.

You love to celebrate the successes of others and feel optimistic about the future, regardless of your current circumstance. When someone does something good, you always applaud them for a job well done. You enjoy making someone's day special, whether it is a child or an adult. You never complain, no matter how unfair your circumstances feel.

You love to be friendly, even with strangers, and often only have to smile to change the mood of a situation. You like to pay everyone well-deserved and sincere compliments. Whenever life knocks you down, you don't hesitate to get up. You understand that relationships mean a great deal more than material things and feel content even not having a lot. In sports or games, you have a great time, even when losing.

It is as if you have a shield that protects you from other people's negativity—it simply doesn't touch or affect you. You love to give; often more than you know you'll get in return. And finally, you always aspire to be no one but yourself.

How did it go? Can you relate to any or all of the qualities above? If not, don't fret. We'll discuss how to overcome a negative mindset in the next section.

Now that we have a better understanding of what a positive mindset entails, we can move on to one of the most important questions of them all: What exactly is the point of possessing a positive mindset? What is it about adopting a positive outlook that is so crucial, so significant, and so life-altering?

The traits and qualities mentioned above provide us with a hint; if you read carefully, you'll find a wealth of advantages connected to positivity, resilience, mental toughness, and mindfulness.

You'll discover that integrity and awareness are related to higher life quality, and that acceptance and thankfulness can help you transition from an "okay life" to a "good life."

Your ability to achieve a truly optimistic mentality and benefit from these things depends on the kind of thoughts you choose to think.

However, this is not the unrealistic kind of positive thinking where everything is positive all the time. Positivity is definitely not justified in every circumstance, every second of the day. At the same time, simply "thinking happy thoughts" won't bring you all the prosperity you desire in life. It's not necessary or possible to always be joyful or upbeat, and cultivating the correct thoughts does not include ignoring anything unpleasant or negative in your life. It's about choosing to remain generally positive while taking both the positive and negative into account.

It involves accepting the fact that you won't always be happy and learning to deal with difficult emotions when they arise. Above all, it's about strengthening your ability to control your attitude toward everything life throws at you. Thoughts do not always stay in your head, and neither can your temperament, but you can decide how to respond to them.

When you decide to give in to pessimism, negativity, and a gloomy outlook on the world, you are not only allowing yourself to lose control and perhaps wallow in misery, but you are also passing up a significant chance for growth and development.

Negative thoughts and feelings have a purpose because they help you focus more intently on risks, vulnerabilities, and dangers. Although possibly not as important as it was for our predecessors, this is essential for survival.

On the other hand, positive thoughts and feelings increase our knowledge and abilities and extend our perspectives. Being cheerful and annoyingly peppy is not the key to developing a favorable mental framework; rather, it requires investing in your future and self. While it's acceptable to experience occasional sadness or pessimism, choosing to respond with optimism, resiliency, and gratitude will serve you much better in the long run.

Developing a positive outlook has numerous other advantages outside of improving your abilities and personal resources, such as improved general health, improved stress management, and increased well-being.

Increased lifespan, decreased rates of depression and distress, increased resistance to the common cold, enhanced psychological and physical well-being, improved cardiovascular health and protection from cardiovascular disease, and the development of coping mechanisms can all be benefits of positive thinking (Mayo Clinic, 2022).

Recognizing Negative Thinking Patterns

Unconscious negative thoughts frequently serve as the trigger for some of our negative behaviors. But how can you become conscious of the thoughts you are having but aren't even aware of?

Luke Thybulle

Recognizing your negative thought patterns can give you the tools you need to stop intrusive thoughts and have a more positive outlook on life. It is possible to alter the negative thought patterns that result in negative emotions and actions and harm your mental toughness, but first, you must learn to identify them.

You often take negative thoughts at face value and don't think to question them, as they tend to be believable. They are intrusive because you did not choose to have them, they can be upsetting or aggressive, and they can be difficult to turn off.

Negative thoughts typically appear automatically without any conscious act on your part. These thoughts will likely be distorted, as they do not match all the facts or are just incorrect. They are unhelpful, in that they have an impact on your emotions and behavior. These thinking patterns make it challenging for you to change and prevent you from achieving your goals in life.

American psychiatrist Aaron Beck discovered that negative thinking followed certain patterns (Ridsdel, 2021). He started to see the emergence of 10 different forms of negative thinking when he visited with his patients and encouraged them to speak openly about their depression and troubles.

Cognitive distortions or "Distorted Thinking" are the terms used to describe these patterns.

Dr. Beck was aware that the negative conclusions or distortions his patients reached were false, contributed to their negative emotions, and did nothing to aid in their recovery. He found that people inadvertently encourage these unreasonable thoughts and beliefs over time. He, therefore, pondered what would happen if his patients could discover how to recognize their distorted thoughts and then flip them. Would confronting these notions help his patients recover?

He created a new technique known as Cognitive Behavioral Therapy, or CBT, to assist with this. He aimed to help people manage their depression, anxiety, and other mental health issues by helping them shift their deeply ingrained, negative perceptions about themselves and the world.

The 10 Cognitive Distortions

In this section, we'll talk about the 10 most common cognitive distortions.

Evaluate whether you tend to fall into one or more of the distortions as you read through each one.

Labeling

When you do something that you or others don't like, you label yourself negatively. You do not recognize or acknowledge that you are not your behavior. Similar to labeling yourself, you write off other people when they act in a way you don't like or make a mistake, as though their actions define who they are.

We'll be using Jill's scenario as an example to further explain these cognitive distortions. If Jill had a negative mindset, what would have happened when Cathy pointed out the flaw in her presentation? Jill would have been upset, probably labeling herself as a failure for overlooking the flaw. She may also have labeled Cathy as a "bad friend" for criticizing her hard work.

Either Magnification or Minimization

An issue can easily be magnified, making it appear larger than it is. Or, perhaps you can minimize both the circumstances and your strengths.

After being made aware of the flaw, Jill could have magnified the situation, gone into a complete panic, and tried to cancel the meeting. Or, she may also have discredited herself by saying something like "I have no skill for preparing presentations!", thus minimizing her own talent.

Mental Filter

You single out one flaw among all the positives and focus all your energy on it but in a negative way.

If Jill experienced cognitive distortion, she may have felt overwhelmed by the single flaw in her presentation, and said something like, "Why do I even bother trying to prepare presentations? I always make mistakes like this!" It would mean that she forgot all about the rest of the presentation which was perfect, only focusing on the fault.

Personalization and Blame Shifting

You blame yourself for circumstances or things over which you have only some degree of control. This distortion is caused by the blame game, which prevents you from considering your own role in the problem when you place the blame on something or someone else.

Instead of finding Cathy's input helpful and working on solving the problem, Jill could have immediately blamed something or someone else. She could have said something like, "Cathy, why didn't you notice the mistake earlier? Why did you wait until I was done?", or, "It's because management expects me to present something that is impossible!"

"Should" Statements

Your perception of how things "should" or "shouldn't" be is crystal clear. You hold yourself or others accountable when they don't work out that way. It's almost like the previous point, except there was a stronger sense of expectation.

Jill could have felt that she wanted to prepare the presentation in a certain way, but somehow rationalizes that she was hindered from doing so. She may have said something like, "I should have seen this mistake, Cathy, if I didn't expect any criticism from you! But I was right! I knew that you'll criticize my work!"

Luke Thybulle

Overgeneralization

You experience something negative, and you start to think that it "always" happens to you. You may also assume something "never" happens to you because you want something to happen but it doesn't. These disturbing ideas create a vicious circle of failure.

Jill could have made herself guilty of overgeneralization when the flaw was pointed out. She could have said something like, "I'll never be able to prepare a great presentation! Cathy, you always see something wrong with my work!"

Emotional Reasoning

You can convince yourself that anything you're feeling has to be true, simply because you're feeling or thinking it.

Instead of seeing Cathy's input as helpful, Jill could have used emotional reasoning to explain what Cathy did. Jill could have said, "Why do you do this to me, Cathy? You're only trying to discourage me from trying!"

Jumping to Conclusions

This is a cognitive distortion that most of us experience, right? How often have you jumped to conclusions without any supporting data, basing your conclusion merely on feelings or thoughts?

Mental Toughness

The moment Cathy pointed out the flaw, Jill could have jumped to a conclusion by assuming to know Cathy's thoughts and intentions, saying something like, "You're just trying to make me nervous so my presentation would be a failure!"

Or, Jill could have assumed to know the outcome of the presentation, and said something like, "Why do I even bother? They're not going to like it anyway!"

All-or-Nothing Thinking

This is about having a black-and-white perspective. There is no gray. You consider something to be a failure if it isn't perfect.

Jill could have felt this way about the flaw, saying something like, "What? There's a flaw? The entire presentation is a failure. I might as well start packing my things. I'm surely going to be fired!"

Discounting the Positive

Due to your tendency to discount positive experiences, you frequently feel inadequate or unappreciated.

Jill might have forgotten all about her positive experiences, saying something like, "Thank you, Cathy, for telling me the presentation is flawed. I'll never prepare a presentation again! I'm no good at it!"

Luke Thybulle

Cathy may then have gently reminded Jill about positive experiences by saying, "But Jill, you have prepared countless presentations before and they all went great. Why else would management expect a presentation from *you*? They know you're the best at it!"

Everyday Habits for Building a Positive Mindset

Before you can start building a positive mindset, you first need to overcome a negative one. According to Dr. Beck, there are five steps required for achieving this (Ridsdel, 2021). Our emotions originate from our thinking. Therefore, in order to change our feelings, we need to change our thoughts.

Overcoming a Negative Mindset

This straightforward-yet-tough formula will reverse these cognitive distortions. The tactics listed below will test each one so you can start to think more rationally and productively. You'll start to feel better as you put these into practice, both about yourself and other people.

First Step: Identify Your Distortions

Start a journal. Take note of which of the 10 Cognitive Distortions you tend to favor as you become more familiar with them. You can keep track of what you're thinking and how you're feeling by recording your thoughts and the related distortions in your journal.

Second Step: Challenge Your Thinking

Because not all of our thoughts are true, it's essential to challenge them. Ask yourself, *is this really true?* while you write down your thoughts and the related distortion. "Do I have any certainty that this is true? Have I verified the facts?"

Take a step back and re-evaluate the circumstance. Ask yourself other difficult questions like "Am I truly a nasty person? or, is it possible that he was doing the best he could and simply made a mistake?" Continue to push your thinking. For example, "how will I know that this is not true?"

Third Step: Compassionate Self-Talk

We are quite hard on ourselves a lot of the time. Our inner dialogue can be harsh, negative, and even abusive. It's likely that you would never say to your friend the things you say to yourself when you consider how you would speak to a good friend.

Write down how you would respond to a good friend for each distortion you've noted. Then, try talking to yourself in a more sympathetic manner by using these responses.

Fourth Step: Seek Support

Locate a trusted friend or another person to assist you in challenging your distortions and assumptions. You can change your perspective from black or white to shades of gray with the correct questions! Thinking more flexibly can help you feel less anxious, nervous, and depressed by reducing your stress levels.

Fifth Step: Positive/Negative Outcomes

To challenge your own cognitive distortions and achieve the mental and emotional freedom you seek, self-evaluation is essential. You can determine if it's worthwhile to keep or change your perspective by allowing yourself to consider the benefits and drawbacks of doing so.

These questions can be helpful:

- *How will believing this distortion benefit or harm me?*

- *Will it take me one step further or one step closer to becoming the person I want to be?*

- *How will my relationship(s) be affected if I stick to my guns and keep thinking the same?*

- *What do I think of myself?*

- *Does allowing this distortion improve or worsen my anxiety, depression, or self-esteem?*

It may take time and effort to challenge your cognitive distortions, but as you take charge of your thoughts rather than letting them rule your life, everything will get so much better.

However, if you find that you are struggling with a severe negative mindset, it's always best to seek the help of a professional.

Cultivating Habits for a Positive Mindset

Those that are positive don't dwell on their issues and obstacles. There is no sea of misery wherever their gaze travels. The other shore is the only option. Those who are positive have a positive outlook, which supports them in leading successful and healthy lives.

Understanding the power of positivity can keep you afloat in the face of catastrophe. Here are four habits you can cultivate to accomplish this.

Positive Affirmations

Positive affirmation is precisely what you'd think it would be: You talk to yourself internally for motivation to perform better. Sometimes, all it takes to fight for your objectives is a little push. You can shift from being a pessimist to becoming an optimist by telling yourself self-favoring phrases. The day when pessimism restricted your life is long gone.

Thinking positively can reduce stress and enhance general health. The advantages can include everything from lower rates of depression to improved adversity resilience. Positive affirmation will decide if anything is a success or a failure. Keep a watchful eye on your inner dialogue. You're setting yourself up for a transformation if your words are inspirational.

Stay in the Present

Those who are positive are rooted in the here and now. They don't dwell on past mistakes or worry incessantly about the future.

Concentrate on your daily tasks in order to bring your wandering thoughts back. Focus on the here and now while doing anything, from doing the dishes to going for a walk. Avoid obsessing about the future or being stuck in the past.

Quit Complaining

First of all, complaining isn't always bad. You occasionally just need to let out some of your frustrations. Also, it demonstrates your ability to recognize problems in your circumstances.

However, if you find yourself complaining all day long, the next step is to change it. Break your procrastinating pattern. You can take baby steps toward it. Instead of feeling down because you haven't been as successful as you'd like, cherish your smaller successes.

Saying "I'm unsuccessful and stupid" is not acceptable. Remind yourself that you've accomplished a lot in your life. Rather say, "I'm pleased with myself."

The trick is to concentrate on what is working well for you; this will help you stop complaining. Thus, if you notice yourself grumbling about something, stop right away and fix your behavior.

If you don't, you might discover that life is progressively difficult. Family and friends may gradually sour. Take the change seriously if you want to avoid it.

Accept the Things You Cannot Change

There are both happy and sad times in life. Expecting positive things to happen all the time would just shatter your heart. The image of what might have been in our heads is what causes havoc in our lives. We are unable to think ahead because we are mired in the past. We all experience both good and terrible days, therefore treat them equally.

The most important thing is how you view the events in your life, even though you can feel worried about them. Life is a journey with many different landscapes and routes. Recognize that some situations are out of your control. You will then enable yourself to enjoy a positive life.

You need a proper dose of positivity to maintain mental toughness. However, if you don't know where you're headed, you may get lost on the way. Therefore, it is essential that you

Luke Thybulle

have effective goals in place, which is what we'll be discussing in the next chapter.

Chapter 5: Setting Realistic and Achievable Goals

These days, the word "goals" is used extensively. So much so that the true nature of its meaning may be unclear. Are goals the same as resolutions and objectives? Why is it important to set goals? Setting goals and succeeding are directly related to one another. Correctly defined goals help inspire new behaviors and help you focus on what's essential to you.

Obviously, it involves more than just setting targets. Accomplishing them is also necessary.

You need to understand what a goal is before you set one. It is something you aspire to accomplish: It is the desired outcome that you or a group of people plan for and firmly resolve to attain.

Still a little puzzled? Here are several traits that explain it.

A goal is:

- Your anticipated future. Setting goals should come after giving considerable thought to your own vision statement and the things you wish to accomplish.

- Large in size and scope. Don't be hesitant to set a challenging goal. Feel free to dream large and think outside the box. You can get there by setting more manageable, immediate targets.

- Time-sensitive. The most successful goals have a deadline. Generally speaking, goals have a longer time range. These can then be divided into more manageable objectives.

A goal is not:

- A mission. Mission statements provide a focused and distinct path to pursue. It is the motivation behind a firm, business, or person's conduct.

- An objective. Objectives are the steps completed to achieve the goal, whereas goals express what you hope to finally accomplish. A goal can sound like: "I wish to develop my public speaking skills". The objective would be, "At the end of this month, I will work with a coach to hone my public speaking abilities."

- A resolution. Resolutions usually only provide short-term gratification (as opposed to delayed gratification). A goal is what you intend to accomplish as opposed to a resolution, which is a decision about whether or not to do something.

Let's talk about the importance of goals, how to set effective ones, and how to plan on achieving them.

The Importance of Goal Setting

Setting goals will eventually result in more tremendous success and fulfillment in all facets of your life. But goal-setting is vital since the process itself has many advantages. These are six rewards for setting goals and persistently working toward them.

Goals Allow You to Achieve More

You enjoy the taste of victory every time you set a goal and achieve it. You'll crave more of that taste of success. Setting goals is a useful method for forming healthy habits.

Why does that matter? You challenge yourself to perform better, push yourself to the next rung on the ladder, and accomplish even more. You can attain far more than you ever imagined by working toward goals, which may often astonish you.

Having Goals Keeps You Motivated

Since there is no stake in the outcome, it is simple to put off tasks until the following day. Let's use an athlete as an example. They will work out every day, whether they feel like it or not, whether they are aching or not, whether they are exhausted or not because they have a goal. They need to get in shape for a competition.

They have a purpose. They aim to perform at a higher level. When they would much rather abscond, they stay in the gym, on the field, or the track because they are driven to reach their goal.

In a similar vein, setting goals will keep you organically driven to perform better!

Goals Inspire Focus

Without a target, your efforts may become scattered and misdirected, which could lead you to forget what it is that you really desire from life.

For instance, a goal can focus your behavior, from that of a hummingbird's chaotic, erratic flight to resemble the focus of a hawk swooping down on its prey.

It enables you to focus with laser accuracy on each day's duties, eliminating unnecessary effort and inactivity.

Goals Aid in Overcoming Procrastination

We all occasionally struggle with procrastination, myself included. Procrastination is harmful, but when you make goals in life—specific goals for what you want to accomplish—it helps you realize that time is being wasted. You aren't getting any closer to your goal when you do nothing.

Goals Allow You to Measure Your Progress

You can only monitor your progress toward a goal if you first set one, which is otherwise impossible. It is incredibly rewarding to monitor your progress toward measurable targets since it will help you stay focused, keep your head held high, and keep your energy levels up. It will also employ preventative psychology concepts by preventing you from being demotivated and averting undesirable results.

When pursuing success, it can be easy to lose motivation because you don't feel like you've "arrived" yet. Although you might not yet be where you want to be, you have taken steps in the right direction and are much better off than when you started, which is something you'll only be aware of when you evaluate your present performance and achievements.

Goals Help You in Deciding What You Want Out of Life

Setting goals makes you think about what you truly want out of life. What level of success are you aiming for? What is your desired amount of income? What does your idea of a good life entail? Where would your ideal house be? What financial requirements do you have to fulfill your dreams?

You can then turn your aspirations into feasible, measurable objectives after you've established these end goals. These targets help you stay motivated, prevent procrastination, and maintain a laser-like concentration on realizing your aspirations. Living your best life is thus made possible through the process of defining, achieving, and surpassing goals.

The scientific community has done substantial research on goal-setting (Tracy, 2022). It has been connected to improved positive emotions, improved academic performance, more team-goal achievement, increased staff engagement, and many other observable advantages.

How to Set Effective and Achievable Goals

Meeting your targets regularly helps keep you motivated and progressing in the direction of your ambitions. However, confidence setbacks can result from goal failure, which makes attainable goals even more essential.

What criteria of goal achievement will help you stay motivated? Below are a few characteristics of goals that are effective and can be achieved.

Build the Skills You Need to Succeed in Your Goals

Reaching your goals involves skills that may take time to master. You must effectively manage your time, exhibit self-discipline, be adaptable, and take on new tasks if you want to succeed.

Say "no" when it's necessary, and keep going when new difficulties arise. Spend time honing soft skills such as problem-solving, work ethic, time management, and adaptability as you press into your goals.

Evaluate Your Goals Each Day

Analyze your daily progress to take stock of your accomplishments. Evaluating your goals may involve tracking certain actions taken, your progress toward your goal, as well as the subsequent results. Did you finish the tasks you set out to do? Were your goals attainable and realistic? Did today's objectives move you one step closer to your long-term goals?

You can maintain focus and strengthen your positive goal-setting habits by monitoring your daily progress and making the necessary corrections. If you didn't complete everything you planned to do today, think about how you can focus more on your goals tomorrow.

Keep It Simple

Continuous and progressive changes are more effective than changing too much at once. Focus your attention on just one or two primary goals at a time.

Goal competition is a problem that might arise when you have too many goals on your mind at once. Goal competition, as its name suggests, occurs when there are too many goals competing for your attention, stealing your time and energy.

Start by deciding on one or two of your most crucial goals. Finally, to help make these demanding targets more manageable, divide them up into smaller components.

Establish a Limit

More is seldom better. Establish a maximum limit of daily goals that you should achieve. For instance, you might want to make at least 15 sales calls every day, but you should also establish a daily cap on the number of outbound calls you'll make in order to maintain balance and prevent burnout.

Your Environment Should Support Your Goals

Unfortunately, we cannot simply will ourselves into good behavior, as we regularly make snap judgments depending on our environment. Create a physical environment that supports your goals to position yourself for success.

Organize and plan, make a vision board, eliminate distractions, surround yourself with positive people, and enjoy affirming media.

Match Your Goals to Your Values

Be sure your goals are consistent with your values before you set them. You will feel comfortable with what you are working so hard for when your goals reflect your values.

Make a list of your core values before setting any specific objectives. Your values may already be clear to you, but knowing what truly matters will help you maintain them at the center of the goals you'll set in order to live the life you want. Spend some time outlining, ranking, and considering what these values truly mean to you.

Our activities are guided by our values, which we live by. Goals that are set outside of our values are hard to achieve.

Include Your Goals in Your Daily Planner

Planning your day in advance increases your chances of achieving your daily aims. Choose a precise time, duration, and location for when you will complete your task whenever you can.

If you like to keep things analogous, acquire a planner that allows you space to organize your meetings and responsibilities each day. Or, use an online daily planner that can notify you of upcoming tasks.

Reward Your Achievements

Reaching a target is an occasion to celebrate. Don't be afraid to treat yourself when you accomplish a goal. As an alternative, punishing yourself for failure has no advantages. Be kind to yourself and focus on the positive development you are making in the long run.

Set SMART Goals

How do SMART goals work? SMART is an acronym and can be broken down into Specific, Measurable, Achievable, Relevant, and Time-bound. Gary Latham and Edwin Locke created the idea (Tracy, 2022).

SMART goals are the five most crucial aspects of goal setting. These five qualities are:

- **Specific:** Be specific about what will be achieved and the precise steps that will be taken.

- **Measurable:** Select data or metrics that will let you know whether or not you are succeeding.

- **Achievable:** Be sure your goals are realistic and that you have the tools and knowledge necessary to achieve them.

- **Relevance:** Verify that the task relates to your long-term goal, values, and life purpose and fits into your overarching objectives.

- **Time-bound:** Set a deadline for finishing your goal and divide it into short-term goals with their own due dates.

Although SMART goals can be challenging, they should also be realistic and achievable. However, you must push yourself and practice self-control to accomplish them.

People are considerably more likely to succeed in their challenging goals if they are clear and have a deadline for fulfillment.

How to Create a Plan for Achieving Your Goals

It's essential that you create a plan to reach your goals since doing so turns an abstract plan into doable actions that support your efforts. Your goals can typically be divided into manageable phases that you can employ to progress toward success. The likelihood of attaining your goals increases when you have concrete actions to pursue.

Find an Interesting Way to Write Down Your Goals

First and foremost, write down your goals. Goal writing is a creative and inspiring activity. Thinking outside the box can occasionally help you describe your objectives in a motivating way. Use a less traditional listing method to see what intentions surface and how you feel you might be able to attain them.

Establish Smaller Milestones Within Your Main Goal, and Celebrate Them

Each goal can be divided into smaller parts. It's critical to acknowledge and celebrate each step that moves you closer to realizing your larger target because doing so can inspire and push you to do the subsequent necessary task.

Clarify Your Goal

It's practically a given that you'll need to modify and redefine your goal as you proceed once you've established it and the steps necessary to attain it. You will be able to repeatedly achieve long-term success throughout your career if you have the agility and capacity to maintain an open mind about how to attain your goals. No good plan is static, so it's crucial to consider any difficulties or roadblocks you might encounter so you can create mitigation and backup strategies.

Your strategy should be flexible and able to change as your situation does. Review your plan frequently so you may adjust it as you go.

Surround Yourself With Motivating People

You become who you associate with. Be deliberate about who you choose to spend your time with because this is true inside and outside of the office. Given that these are the kinds of traits that have an impact on your own behaviors and attitudes, you should surround yourself with ambitious, organized, and helpful people.

In order to protect your desire to pursue your goals, be sure to set aside time and space from any people who, for whatever reason, you feel are having a detrimental effect on your motivation. Your time is too valuable to be wasted with people who obstruct your development or achievement.

Establish Realistic Expectations

Be truthful to yourself. You will be discouraged from working toward your goal if it is unattainable. As a result, it's crucial to divide your targets into more manageable, concrete steps. Being realistic makes you more responsible because you are confident in your ability to do these tasks. Not only do the minor tasks that add up to form your aims need to be viable and realistic, but so must your schedule and resource list.

If you begin goal-setting with inflated expectations, you'll find it difficult to stay motivated and you can run into more difficulties in the long term in achieving your goals. Being realistic with yourself is considerably simpler and more effective.

Identify the Resources You'll Require

In addition to deciding what you'll do to achieve a certain goal, you also need to decide what resources are required to succeed. Consider whether the desired outcome calls for specific tools, technology, materials, or funding. Your action plan differs from a wish list due to the allocation of resources.

Making decisions on how to carry out each step necessary to attain your targets will become possible once you have identified the resources required to do so. Create a list of resources you think are necessary to achieve your targets, then give it to your employer or the other team members you're working with.

Inform Others About Your Goal

Share your goal with others so that they can encourage you while you try to attain it. There is no question that trustworthy colleagues, friends, and others will do everything in their power to assist you when they are aware of your goals. Setting individual aims with your manager is a wonderful approach to letting them know what you're working toward and to getting their advice and support.

Prioritize Your Goals

Knowing which goals should be prioritized is crucial since different goals call for various planning strategies. In this situation, you should first decide what, in terms of priority, you would like to accomplish first. Making lists is an excellent method to visualize your priorities and the timescales for each one.

Mental Toughness

When you prioritize your duties and goals, and give them set due dates, your action plan becomes substantially more workable. You can determine the actions necessary to get there by arranging the outcomes you wish to attain. This prioritizing is especially important if you're working in a team to ensure accountability.

Assign Progress Deadlines

Setting clear deadlines for yourself will help you stay organized and on course to meet your goals. This method is very helpful when you need to manage your time well while working on multiple things at once.

Progress deadlines not only aid in time management, but they also enable you to hold yourself accountable for completing the targets that you set for yourself. You may keep organized and on track to meeting your objectives by breaking down larger goals and giving them due dates.

Track Your Progress

When you try to accomplish your goals, it's crucial to monitor your progress. Your objectives and key results (OKRs) should be documented, defined, and monitored so you always know what has been done and what needs to be done. Tracking your progress is ideal, whether discussing your accomplishments and development with your supervisor in one-on-one meetings or team meetings.

Luke Thybulle

Everyday Habits for Achieving Your Goals

According to research, 45% of Americans generally set New Year's resolutions, but only 8% of them are actually achieved (Halvorson, 2015). What is it that distinguishes those 8%? It may seem straightforward, but it all boils down to their habits.

If you want to accomplish your goals, try developing the following habits:

Recognize That All Qualities Can Be Enhanced

When they believe they aren't capable of achieving their goals, some people become demoralized and give up. Those who succeed understand that this is untrue; even personality or intelligence can improve with time. You'll succeed more easily if you make it a habit to improve all of your qualities.

Make It a Habit to Persevere

The adage "When the going gets tough, the tough get going" is a way of life for people who routinely succeed in their goals. They mentally get ready to push through by acknowledging how challenging the road to their goals will be. If you want to be someone who achieves their goals, having the habit of perseverance is crucial.

Mental Toughness

Adopt Better Habits in Place of Harmful Ones

Setting a goal to do something new is far more efficient than setting a goal to quit doing something. If you want to break a bad habit, concentrate on developing a new behavior for that circumstance. Instead of declaring, "I'll never become angry at my child," try saying, "When I feel furious at my child, I'll pause for 10 seconds before speaking." This way, you are creating a habit that is positive and specific.

Stop Making Excuses

When they don't succeed, many people end up making excuses. Successful people don't hide behind excuses; rather, they view failures as an opportunity to re-evaluate and try again. Make it a habit to resist giving in to excuses and instead empower yourself to continue working toward your target.

Be Humble About Your Skills

The people who are most successful in achieving their goals are aware that there is always room for improvement through learning and growing. They can accept assistance and repeatedly produce achievement by remaining humble and teachable.

Having goals means you have a direction to move into. Teamed with mental toughness, you'll be an unstoppable force! As we discussed in this chapter, there is always potential for improvement. Therefore, we'll talk about enhancing your emotional intelligence in the next chapter.

Luke Thybulle

Chapter 6: Building Emotional Intelligence

The capacity to recognize, use, and regulate your own emotions in order to reduce stress, communicate clearly, empathize with others, overcome obstacles, and diffuse conflict is known as emotional intelligence, or emotional quotient (EQ) (Segal et al., 2020). You can develop stronger relationships, perform well at work and school, and reach your professional and personal goals with the aid of emotional intelligence. Additionally, it can assist you in establishing a connection with your emotions, putting your intentions into practice, and choosing what is most important to you.

Understanding Emotional Intelligence

Your EQ is just as important as your IQ when it comes to fulfillment and achievement in life. This chapter will teach you how to increase your emotional intelligence, forge stronger bonds with others, and accomplish your goals.

The Constructs of Emotional Intelligence

Four constructs are typically used to characterize emotional intelligence:

Self-awareness

This refers to an awareness of how your own emotions impact your thoughts and actions. This makes it easier to be confident in yourself and aware of your strengths and weaknesses.

How would Jill have reacted when Cathy pointed out the flaw in her presentation if she had low levels of emotional intelligence? She probably would have doubted herself and her skills to prepare an effective presentation. But because Jill was aware of her own strengths and weaknesses, she was able to accept Cathy's input as constructive criticism and was able to correct the flaw in the presentation. She did not allow self-doubt to take over, as she knew and acknowledged that she was good at preparing presentations.

Relationship Management

Is the understanding of how to establish and maintain positive relationships, communicate effectively, motivate and influence people, collaborate effectively with others, and handle conflict.

Jill clearly showed signs of emotional intelligence, as she valued the relationship with her friend, enough to understand that she only had her best interest at heart. Cathy felt that she could point out the flaw, as Jill's behavior cultivated a sense of security in her around the importance of their friendship.

Self-management

You possess the capacity to restrain impulsive thoughts and actions, regulate your emotions in healthy ways, exercise initiative, keep your word, and adjust to changing situations.

Imagine for a moment that Jill lacked self-management. What would she have said or done when Cathy pointed out the flaw? She may have seen it as an attack on her person and retaliated. But Jill didn't. She restrained herself, realized that she was now facing a changing situation, and adapted accordingly.

Social Awareness

You're empathetic. You are able to discern emotional indicators, comprehend the needs and worries of others, feel at ease in social situations, and comprehend the power dynamics in a team or organization.

Although Jill fully trusted her own skills, she recognized that it couldn't hurt to accept necessary input from a friend. She understood the dynamics of teamwork and, although initially taken aback, was grateful for Cathy's input.

We all know that the most successful and content individuals are not necessarily the most intellectual. Conversely, you probably know someone who excels academically but is socially awkward and unproductive at work or in personal relationships. Your intelligence quotient (IQ) or intellectual prowess is insufficient on its own to lead a successful life.

Sure, your IQ can help you get an education, but your emotional intelligence (EQ) is what will enable you to control your stress and emotions as you approach your final examinations. IQ and EQ go hand in hand and work best when they complement one another.

Areas That Are Affected by Emotional Intelligence

Let's talk about the areas in life that are heavily affected by emotional intelligence. See how many of these you can relate to. If not, no problem! Emotional intelligence can be developed and enhanced. But first, let's look at the areas.

Relationships

You are better able to articulate how you feel and comprehend how others are feeling if you have improved awareness of your emotions and how to control them. As a result, you can build deeper relationships in both your personal and professional life and communicate more effectively.

Jill's relationships were affected by emotional intelligence. Do you agree? This helped her to understand that Cathy's input was not negative criticism or an attack. Jill understood how Cathy was feeling, respected her for it, and accepted her advice.

Your Academic or Professional Performance

You can lead and inspire people, succeed in your profession, and negotiate the social complexity of the workplace with high emotional intelligence. In fact, many businesses now prioritize emotional intelligence above technical competence when evaluating key job prospects and conduct EQ tests before hiring.

Emotional intelligence is probably why management asked Jill to create the presentation. They most likely knew her skills and were aware that she understood the social complexity of the workplace.

Your Mental Well-Being

Stress and unchecked emotions can negatively affect your mental health and put you at risk for depression and anxiety. Strong connections will be difficult for you to establish if you are unable to comprehend, accept, or manage your emotions. This can further aggravate existing mental health issues and leave you feeling isolated and alone.

If Jill had a low level of emotional intelligence, disappointment and anger could have easily taken over. Instead, Jill kept a cool head, didn't allow herself to become anxious, and gracefully adjusted her presentation in full regard to Cathy's input.

Your Physical Well-Being

If you can't control your emotions, it's likely that you can't control your stress either. Serious health issues may result from this. Unmanaged stress increases blood pressure, weakens the immune system, boosts the risk of heart attacks and strokes, affects fertility, and hastens aging. Learning how to control your stress is the first step to increasing your emotional intelligence.

I think it is safe to say that Jill takes care of her physical well-being, not allowing stress or anxiety to overrun her mind. This can also be a reason she is requested to prepare presentations—her physical well-being allows her to be trustworthy.

Social Intelligence

Understanding your emotions helps you connect with others and the outside world on a social level. You can discern a friend from an enemy, gauge another person's interest in you, relieve stress, regulate your nervous system through social interaction, and feel loved and happy because of social intelligence.

Jill was able to distinguish a friend from an enemy, in that she knew Cathy meant well by pointing out the flaw. She understood that, if Cathy kept quiet, management would have probably noticed it and it could have been detrimental to her career. So, instead of being angered or panicked, Jill was grateful for Cathy's input.

How does emotional intelligence impact your life? Is there room for change or improvement, or both? But first, let's talk about what EQ has to do with mental toughness.

How Emotional Intelligence Relates to Mental Toughness

People give up mentally before their physical resources fail in most stressful situations. In addition to physical prowess, mental and emotional stamina are the keys to great performance. Excellence comes from mastering grit, resilience, coping, adaptability, and toughness. Everyone encounters stress, failures, disappointments, challenges, adversity, and the downsides of life, but emotional intelligence makes it possible to become a tough target.

Inner fortitude can triumph. "Can't" is far less frequent than "won't." Being mentally tough requires an active mentality and belief system. They are proactive answers that transform reactions.

The fundamental component is emotional intelligence. Without the capacity to completely comprehend, accept, and act upon intensely negative feelings, one falls short of being mentally tough. Events that put your mental toughness to the test ultimately put your emotional intelligence to the test.

Mentally strong people have an internal arsenal of tools they can use to handle any difficulties from the outside world. They have developed successful habits from the fundamental traits. They take an effort to actively develop the proactive and responsive tools they require, starting with an attitude of self-reliance.

While positive, constructive development should be prioritized, it is crucial to stay away from the dangers of negative traits and unproductive habits. Patterns disintegrate if they are not consciously maintained. They deteriorate into disorder, clutter, and ineffective habits.

Luke Thybulle

Positive perspectives on satisfaction, happiness, optimism, and opportunity are the emphasis of emotional intelligence.

Being emotionally strong (tough, grit, resilient, adaptable, and having coping mechanisms) is not an all-or-nothing proposition. It has to do with the heart, mind, and body, as they are all innately linked. There are different, independent levels in each of the three sections. Growing in all areas leads to building mental toughness and coping skills.

The individual has carried out the necessary preparations and is at the readiness level. The initiation is the true catalyst which enables resolve, routines, and habits to be persistently formed. Competence is built on a foundation of conscious skills, which means the journeyman possesses the capability to function at a high level. Masters attain true excellence and subconsciously relaxed competence at the greatest levels.

The nine Cs are the key competencies in sports, professionalism, and all other facets of life. They are dynamic, actively developed soft skills that strengthen the system. The C's stand for:

- Commitment
- Consistency
- Challenge
- Concentration
- Character
- Courage
- Control

- Composure

- Confidence

The pattern of mental toughness extends from overcoming minor challenges to managing major events. The proactive tools that turn many issues into fleeting troubles and opportunities are inner strength and tenacity. Adaptability and coping mechanisms are put front and center when shifts or transitions are the best course of action. Resilience and recovery are the solutions to setbacks. Emotional intelligence, perspective, optimism, and the application of these abilities are the keys to mental toughness.

It's not just about dealing with problems; it's also about having the mindset to overcome challenges.

According to Bob Jerus, founder of Success Dynamics International, there are six levels for mastering emotional intelligence (Jerus, 2018). Throughout, one can clearly see how the mind, heart, and body are intertwined. Let's investigate these levels.

Readiness

This is the first level and indicates that the person is ready for change.

Luke Thybulle

Mind

The person has adopted a growth mindset and shows a lot of interest. They like to study and learn new things, and are curious and love to explore.

Heart

Their hearts are filled with positivity. They prefer constructive engagements and want to be committed and experience happiness.

Body

They are ready to live a healthy lifestyle, and likely aim to become fit. This will provide them with the energy and vitality they need. They want things to be balanced and aim to strengthen themselves physically and mentally.

Initiation

This is the second level when the person decides to step out of their comfort zone and adopt change.

Mind

The individual is aware of their purpose. They know how to set priorities. They have an agenda and a program ready. Excitement fills them for what the future holds causing them to live with drive.

Heart

They are becoming more aware of their environment and themselves. The world is filled with wonderful things for them to discover. They don't need to be prompted and love to take initiative. They do not lack imagination and are innovative. They know how to define what they want out of life and understand making the best of their weaknesses, strengths, and circumstances.

Body

They are more interested in physical activity. They understand the benefits of conditioning and having a regimen. They welcome challenges with rigor.

Persistence

The third level indicates that the person is set on regaining control and refuses to quit.

Luke Thybulle

Mind

The person shows a strength of character. They persevere with courage and fortitude. High levels of resilience are evident and are aimed at mental and physical recovery and well-being.

Heart

They are interested in a healthy and positive perspective. They live with resolve and relentless dedication. Their passion is continually growing stronger.

Body

They are careful about their diet and welcome healthy and nutritious food, as well as remaining hydrated. They are fully aware of the benefits of getting enough rest and display an increase in stamina. Their physical improvement leads to the improvement of all relationships.

Competence

This is the fourth level which can be tough to reach.

Mind

The individual is in control of their mind, body, and spirit. They understand the benefits of being relaxed and quiet. They are unshaken by internalized values. They can easily be identified as they are the ones who have a "can-do" mindset.

Heart

The individual experiences an integration of body, mind, and heart. These aspects are intertwined and drive one another. They have a positive attitude and understand the importance of having good fun.

Body

They know how to manage their energy and are in the process of replacing harmful or non-beneficial habits with constructive habits. Life is tackled with tenacity and endurance.

Journeyman

In this fifth level, the individual is well on their way to solid emotional intelligence.

Mind

The person knows how to set goals and achieve them. They are focused with their minds set on productivity and quality.

Heart

They feel self-satisfied and fulfilled as their purpose and passion are aligned.

Body

They are highly agile and interested in honing their skills. They are set on performing at their best and improving wherever possible.

Mastery

This is the sixth level—the individual has mastered emotional intelligence!

Mind

Success comes nearly effortlessly as the person lives with unconscious excellence. They are in full control of their inner dialogue. They know how to visualize a bright future and formulate plans before setting goals to achieve this.

Heart

They have adopted a lifestyle that is beneficial for their mental and physical health, and constantly strive for satisfaction and contentment. To them, life is about quality.

Body

Their routines are set on measurable and meaningful results, focused on achieving success. They don't simply believe in dreams; but in actualization.

Everyday Habits for Building Emotional Intelligence

We now know what emotional intelligence is, what it looks like, and how it relates to mental toughness. However, the question may remain—how do I enhance my emotional intelligence? Let's talk about habits you can implement to successfully achieve this.

Expressiveness

Even if they are empaths and aware of their feelings, some people find it difficult to express them to others. Not only do emotionally intelligent people understand emotions, but they also know how to express them appropriately.

What does it mean to express them appropriately? Consider this scenario: You just experienced a terrible day at work. You're unhappy about how things went at a crucial meeting and you're also exhausted and annoyed. Coming home and fighting with your partner or writing a scathing email to your boss are examples of unacceptable ways to vent your emotions.

Cultivate this habit: Discuss your frustrations with your partner, unwind with a jog, and formulate a goal to improve the next day. These all would lead to more suitable emotional responses.

Self-Regulation

Self-regulation is closely related to expressiveness but is about a lifestyle rather than having emotional outbursts.

The foundation of emotional intelligence is self-regulation. Being aware of your emotions is fantastic, but it won't help you much if you don't put it to use. Those that are emotionally intelligent consider their actions before acting on emotions. They are conscious of their feelings, but they do not let them control how they live.

Cultivate this habit: Take time to identify and assess your emotions before you react. Make a conscious decision that your emotions will not overpower or alter your mindset.

Social Skills

Because they are so sensitive to their own emotions as well as those of others, emotionally intelligent people typically have good social skills. They are skilled in interpersonal communication and committed to upholding positive social bonds and supporting individuals in their immediate vicinity.

Cultivate this habit: Hone your sensitivity by spending time with people. Try to analyze their thoughts and feelings. Find ways to relay these to them and see if you are correct. However, do this without being intrusive. If someone confides in you, tell them what you think they are feeling. They can then let you know if you are right on the mark, or if you should adjust or improve your skills.

Empathy

Another crucial component of EQ is empathy. You need to be able to understand other people's emotions in order to interact with them in a variety of life contexts, such as at work or school. Knowing what a coworker is feeling can help you respond to them more effectively if they are irritated or frustrated.

Cultivate this habit: Understanding other people's emotions can take time to master. Before you react, place yourself in that person's shoes. Imagine what they must be feeling. Then, if necessary, respond.

Motivation

People with emotional intelligence are driven to succeed in their goals. They have the capacity to control their emotions and behaviors in order to succeed in the long run.

They may feel anxious about making changes in their lives, but they are aware of the need to control their anxiety. They realize that by taking risks and changing, they can improve their lives and get a little bit closer to their goals.

Cultivate this habit: Whenever the need arises to set another goal, decide that you will remain motivated. It can be hard, therefore, if you feel your energy is running low, take a breather. Relax, recharge, and then resume.

Self-Awareness

Self-awareness includes the capacity to identify one's own feelings, emotions, and moods. Being conscious of your impact on other people's emotions and moods is a component of self-awareness. A fundamental necessity for emotional intelligence is the capacity to keep track of your own emotional states.

Cultivate this habit: Be mindful of your emotions. Assess them and decide whether a certain emotion is helpful or harmful. Let go of the emotions that will serve no purpose, even if you feel justified to be angry or upset. Realize that emotions often go as quickly as they come, which is why a lot of people live with regret for how they responded at some point.

Perceptiveness

Picture yourself being upset and annoyed with a coworker. Examine the source of your genuine distress as you evaluate your feelings. Do you feel angry because of your coworker's behavior, or is it caused by pressure from your supervisor or too much work and responsibilities on your plate?

Those with emotional intelligence are able to consider the circumstances and accurately pinpoint the underlying cause of their emotions. This may appear to be a simple activity at first, but in actuality, our emotional life may be messy and complex. It can be difficult to pinpoint the exact cause of your emotions when dealing with strong emotions like love or anger.

Cultivate this habit: Whenever you feel angry, upset, or annoyed, ask yourself why you are feeling that way. Take the other person out of the picture and focus on yourself. I'm not saying that you should find fault with yourself, but we often experience unnecessary emotions triggered by memories of past traumatic or hurtful events.

In this chapter, you have frequently seen that you must assess and control your emotions. If you don't know how, don't worry. In the next chapter, we'll talk about how you can master your emotions and handle stress.

Luke Thybulle

Chapter 7: Managing Stress and Emotions

Stress is a normal reaction to feeling unable to handle particular demands or circumstances. But, if a person does not take action to control it, stress can develop into a chronic condition. These demands may originate from the workplace, interpersonal connections, financial strains, or other circumstances. Nonetheless, stress can be brought on by anything that presents a genuine or perceived challenge or threat to one's well-being.

Stress can spur motivation and even be necessary for survival. The fight-or-flight response system in the body instructs a person on when and how to react to danger. Yet, it can affect a person's physical and mental health if the body is too easily triggered or when there are too many stresses present at once.

Stress serves as the body's natural protection against danger and predators. Hormones that prime the body to avoid or face danger are released in a rush when this happens. This is sometimes referred to as the fight-or-flight response.

When confronted with a challenge or threat, humans display a partially physical response. The body mobilizes resources to either stay and face the threat or flee as quickly as possible.

The levels of the hormones, cortisol, adrenaline, and norepinephrine increase in the body. They result in the following physiological responses:

- muscles are prepared for action

- the individual is on high alert

- there's an increase in blood pressure

- the individual may be sweating profusely

All of these elements enhance a person's capacity to react in a potentially dangerous or challenging circumstance. The release of norepinephrine and epinephrine also quickens the heart rate.

Stressors are the external stimuli that cause this reaction. Examples include loud noises, aggressive behavior, a moving vehicle at high speeds, frightful movie sequences, or even going on a first date. With a greater number of stressors, stress levels tend to rise as well.

Stress does not only affect the body but the mind as well. In the next section, we'll talk about how stress affects our mental toughness. Then, we'll also look at habits that will help us manage stress and regulate our emotions.

Understanding the Effects of Stress on Mental Toughness

In recent times, stress-related disorders have significantly increased as a result of managing rising emotional and social demands, as well as the difficulty of modernizing corporate methods. And over the upcoming months and years, this can be expected to continue.

Organizations have an ethical duty to provide assistance to their employees so that stress's damaging effects on their welfare and mental health can be lessened. Being effective on a personal and professional level all depends on our ability to effectively regulate our emotions as well as those of others.

People may not receive the same degree of support, social interactions, or opportunities if they are required to work from home as they had imagined. Isolation and low morale may result from this experience. So, it's critical for leaders to spot younger team members and provide additional assistance through regular check-ins regarding their welfare and open discussions about their goals.

The sense of losing control over one's environment lies at the heart of all stress-related disorders. Furthermore, the stress of losing control results in a generalized anxiety response. This is especially important to organizations that are having trouble dealing with problems brought on by increased complexity and stress at work.

People's interest in someone's capacity to exert control over their own emotional state may not come as a surprise. And one of the sources of mental wellness is the perception of control. Gaining mental toughness promotes a calm mind, access to pleasant emotions, and helpful behaviors by diminishing the influence of anger or worry.

The capacity to cultivate a serene mind is among the most crucial abilities you need in order to be able to lead well in both your personal and professional life. It's challenging to think clearly and impossible to come up with original ideas when you're under pressure and your mind is clouded by stress.

To develop strong judgment and make clear decisions at work, it is essential to be able to keep your composure under constant pressure. So, to effectively lead in any modern organization, mindfulness is a necessary ability.

Moreover, compared to past generations, emerging generations claim to have different expectations of leadership. Instead of establishing power based on hierarchy, they choose leaders who are emotionally intelligent, self-aware, and capable of inspiring others. They are more excited about consensus leadership styles and want to be involved in decision-making.

Develop the emotional skills of mental toughness to reduce pervasive anxiety and improve decision-making, executive control, clinical outcomes, and professional success. Leaders with emotional self-control can control their emotions under pressure and exude confidence to others around them.

Highly self-controlled leaders can respond to difficult circumstances as opposed to simply reacting to them. With their support of the vulnerable and their protection of staff from the repercussions of ambiguity and uncertainty, mentally tough leaders serve as shock absorbers in an organization.

Keeping your mind at ease is therefore one of your most important daily goals in order to lessen the negative consequences of stress and added strain. It is increasingly essential to include emotional intelligence and mental toughness in corporate cultures.

Mental Toughness

However, this is not only true in the corporate world, but also in sports and personal life. A mentally tough parent is more capable of handling their child's anxieties. Of course, there are other stresses to consider, such as financial, career-related, and social issues.

While it is true that all people experience stress at some point, the levels we experience vary greatly. The way we have been educated by our parents, family members, friends, and teachers also have an impact on how we manage stress.

But here's the problem—imagine being constantly battered by issues that cause stress and anxiety. Yes, we know we should be mentally tough, but this requires effort and energy. It may happen that a person runs out of energy and ends up feeling like a wave being tossed around at sea, even if they are mentally tough.

We typically don't ask for negative things that come our way. We have no control over that. People who are there to support you can only do so much. This means that stress can end up being detrimental to your mental toughness.

How do you remain energized and motivated if you feel like the universe's punching bag? Staying calm and analyzing your situation may be easier said than done.

How can you prevent your mental toughness from being harmed or destroyed? Can you even do that? What if life is simply too hard to remain mentally tough?

The good news is that, while you may feel beaten down, you don't have to succumb to despair. There is hope! Let's imagine that you're a pig farmer. I think it's a no-brainer that pigs need to be kept in a pen or an enclosure, or yes, a pigsty. What would happen if you left the gate open? You'll be running around, exhausting yourself trying to catch them all, right?

The same thing happens to your thoughts and feelings. If you leave the gate open just a little, they'll come running out, and you'll have to go into a frenzy to find them and put them back where they belong. Let's see what you can do to keep all your, well, pigs in their sty.

Everyday Habits for Managing Stress

Stress can have an impact both mentally and physically, which means managing it will be beneficial to your mind and body. The chaos in your life can be brought back to order with the use of stress relievers. Stress relievers don't require a lot of effort or thought. Try some of these suggestions if your stress is out of control and you need immediate relief.

Make Some Music and Use Your Creativity

Playing or listening to music can help you relax because it can divert your attention from your worries, remove tension in your muscles, and lower your stress levels. Turn the music up loud and allow yourself to be lost in it.

If music isn't your thing, focus on anything else you like to do, like gardening, sewing, or drawing—anything that makes you concentrate on what you're doing rather than what you think you should be doing. Or, you can do both! Imagine creating a serene portrait while listening to Led Zeppelin, or whichever artist you prefer.

Give Yoga a Chance

Yoga is a well-liked method of reducing stress thanks to its array of positions and controlled breathing techniques. Yoga combines mental and physical disciplines that can aid in achieving mental and physical harmony. You can control your anxiety and stress by practicing yoga.

You may find courses in most areas, or you can try yoga on your own. Because of its slower tempo and simpler motions, hatha yoga in particular, is effective for reducing stress, which means you don't need the skills to fold yourself into a pretzel. Anyone can do it.

Bolster Your Sense of Humor

Even if you have to fake laugh through your grumpiness, a strong sense of humor can make you feel better, even if not for all conditions. Laughing not only helps you feel better mentally, but it also has a great physical impact on your body. So, go ahead and deliver jokes, read jokes, watch comedies, or just hang out with your hilarious friends. Perhaps attempt laughter yoga (yes, that's a thing).

Luke Thybulle

Start Journaling

Putting your ideas and feelings into writing might help you let go of otherwise bottled-up emotions. Don't ponder what to write; simply let it come to you. Whatever comes to mind, write it. You don't need anyone else to read it, so don't worry about spelling or punctuation.

Simply let your ideas flow onto a piece of paper or a computer screen. When you're through, you can either throw away what you wrote or store it for further reflection.

Enjoy a Balanced Diet

And with *that,* I don't mean having a chocolate bar in both hands. Maintaining a nutritious diet is a crucial aspect of self-care. Eat a variety of fruits, vegetables, whole grains, and other healthy foods.

Stand Your Ground

Even though you might want to, you can't accomplish it all, at least not without having to pay a price. You can better control your to-do list and your stress by developing the ability to say no or by being willing to delegate.

It may appear simple to say yes in order to maintain harmony, avert confrontation, and complete the task at hand. The fact that your needs and those of your family are put aside, however, may actually cause you inner turmoil. This can result in stress, anger, resentment, and even the desire to seek retribution. And that's not a very collected and serene response.

Try Meditation

You don't need to flee to an isolated mountain top to meditate, nor do you have to adopt a different religion. Everyone can do this, too. You can silence the constant stream of disorganized ideas that may be stressing you out by focusing your attention during meditation. Both your mental well-being and your general health can benefit from the sense of calm, peace, and balance that meditation can help you achieve.

Whether you're taking a walk, taking the bus to work, or waiting at the doctor's office, you can practice guided meditation, guided imagery, visualization, and other types of meditation anywhere, at any time. Anywhere you want is a good place to try deep breathing.

Get Moving

Almost any physical exercise has the ability to reduce stress. Exercise can be an effective stress reliever even if you're not athletic or in good physical form.

Exercise can increase your levels of feel-good endorphins and other natural neurotransmitters that improve your mood. Exercise can also help you refocus your attention on how your body is moving, which can boost your mood and help you forget about the day's discomforts. Take into account activities that get you moving, such as walking, swimming, running, gardening, biking, housecleaning, weightlifting, or anything else. As long as you're moving, you're doing great!

Get Adequate Sleep

Stress might make it difficult to fall asleep. Sleep can suffer when you have too much to accomplish or too much to think about. Nevertheless, sleep is the time your brain and body regenerate.

Furthermore, the quality and quantity of sleep you obtain might have an impact on your mood, energy level, focus, and overall functioning. If you're having difficulties sleeping, make sure you have a calm, relaxing night routine, listen to soothing music, turn off clocks, and stick to a steady schedule.

Connect With Other People

When you're stressed and cranky, it's natural to want to withdraw yourself. Instead, strengthen your social relationships with family and friends.

Social contact is an effective stress reliever since it can divert, support, and help you tolerate the ups and downs of life. So, go for a coffee break with a friend, send an email to a relative, or pay a visit to your place of worship.

Do you have additional time? Try volunteering for a charitable organization to benefit yourself while also benefiting others.

Don't Behave Badly

Some people cope with stress by overindulging in caffeine or alcohol, smoking, overeating, or using illegal substances. These behaviors can be harmful to your mental and physical health. If you find that you have adopted some bad habits, eliminate them by replacing them with wholesome and beneficial habits. There's no shame if you need help to do so, which leads us to the next and final habit.

Find Counseling

You might need to look for reinforcements in the form of therapy or counseling if new stressors are making it difficult for you to manage or if self-care techniques aren't working. Counseling may also be a good idea if you feel confined or overburdened, worry excessively, or struggle to complete everyday tasks or fulfill obligations at work, home, or school.

You can acquire new coping mechanisms and identify the causes of your stress with the aid of qualified counselors or therapists, thereby also maintaining your mental toughness.

Everyday Habits for Regulating Your Emotions

You might be able to regulate your emotions without repressing or exerting control over them. Your relationships, attitude, decision-making, and mental toughness can all benefit from this. Let's look at some habits you can cultivate to keep your emotions in check.

Keep Stress Under Control

This ties in with the previous section. It can be challenging to control your emotions when you're under a lot of stress. Even those who typically have good emotional self-control may find it more difficult to do so under conditions of extreme stress and tension.

Your emotions can become more controllable by reducing stress or learning more effective stress-management techniques, such as discussed in the previous section. Meditation and other mindfulness techniques can reduce stress as well. They may not eliminate it, but they can make it more bearable.

Know When You Can Express Yourself Freely

For everything, including strong emotions, there is a proper time and place. For instance, crying uncontrollably after losing a loved one is a fairly typical reaction. After being dumped, you might find that screaming or even pounding your pillow will help you release some of your anger and stress.

But in some circumstances, moderation is required. Screaming at your supervisor over an unfair disciplinary action won't solve anything, no matter how furious you are.

You can learn when to express your feelings and when you might want to sit with them for the time being by being aware of your surroundings and the scenario.

Accept and Acknowledge All of Your Emotions

You may try downplaying your feelings to yourself since you want to improve your ability to control your emotions.

It may seem beneficial to tell yourself, "Just stay calm," or "It's not that big of an issue, so don't stress out," when you begin to hyperventilate after receiving wonderful news or collapse on the floor weeping and shouting when you can't locate your keys.

Yet, this discredits your experience. To you, it is really important.

You can become more at ease with your emotions if you accept them as they are. You may feel intense emotions more thoroughly and avoid extreme, counterproductive reactions by increasing your comfort level with them.

Try viewing emotions as messengers to practice accepting them. They are neither good nor bad. They're neutral. Even if they occasionally trigger difficult feelings, they are still providing you with useful information.

For instance, try: "I'm annoyed because I constantly misplace my keys, which causes me to be late. To help me remember to leave them in the same spot, I should put a dish on the shelf by the door."

Luke Thybulle

More life contentment and fewer mental health symptoms can result from accepting emotions. Also, thinking of emotions as helpful can result in higher levels of enjoyment in people.

Consider the Impact of Your Emotions

Not all strong emotions are bad. Our lives are made intriguing, distinctive, and lively by emotions. Intense emotions can be an indication that we truly embrace life and aren't suppressing our innate responses.

Whether something fantastic, tragic, or something you feel like you've missed out on happens, it's completely normal to sometimes feel emotionally overwhelmed.

So, how can you recognize an issue when it arises?

Frequent irrational emotions can result in:

- emotional or physical outbursts
- conflict in a friendship or relationship
- complications at work or school
- a desire to use substances to assist you to manage your emotions
- a problem connecting with people

Take some time to evaluate how your uncontrolled emotions are impacting your daily life. Problem areas will be simpler to spot as a result (and to track your success).

Meditation

If you already meditate, it might be one of your go-to strategies for handling strong emotions. You can become more conscious of all emotions and experiences by practicing meditation. In doing so, you're teaching yourself to sit with those emotions and recognize them without criticizing or trying to modify or suppress them.

Emotional control can be made simpler by learning to accept all of your emotions, as was already indicated. You can improve these acceptance skills by meditating. Other advantages include improving your ability to unwind and sleep better.

Breathe

Whether you're exuberantly joyful or furiously upset and unable to speak, there is much to be said about the power of taking a deep breath.

Although, slowing down and focusing on your breathing won't make unpleasant emotions go away, practicing deep breathing can help you center yourself, take a step back from the initial, overwhelming emotion, and any excessive reaction you'd rather avoid.

Next time your emotions begin to overwhelm you, do the following:

- Inhale deeply. The diaphragm, not the chest, is where deep breaths originate. Visualizing your breath rising from your abdomen may be of aid.

- Retain it. Hold your breath for three counts, then exhale slowly.

- Think of a mantra. Repetition of a mantra, such as "I am peaceful" or "I am relaxed," can be beneficial for some people.

Identify Your Emotion

You may start taking back control by taking a moment to tune in with your mood.

Let's go back to Jill once more. Jill was thrilled with the presentation she had created and hoped her friend Cathy would feel the same way.

But she identified a problem with the presentation when Jill showed it to her.

Jill was startled, but she could have been furious. She might have thrown her phone across the room, tipped over her trash can, and kicked her desk, stubbing her toe, all without pausing to think.

Instead, she stopped and asked herself:

- What am I currently feeling? (Unhappy, irate, and furious.)

- What took place to give me this feeling? (Cathy pointed out an error she saw in my presentation.)

- Does an alternate explanation for the circumstance exist that would make sense? (It may be that Cathy has my best interest at heart. I mean, if she hadn't called attention to the error, management would have undoubtedly found it.)

- What do I want to do in response to these emotions? (Scream, hurl objects to express my rage, or say something rude.)

- Is there a more effective method of handling them? (Express appreciation for the suggestions and see if she has any more to add. It may help if I take a walk or drink some tea first.)

You can change your first, extreme response by reframing your thinking to take into account potential alternatives.

It could take some time before this reaction becomes ingrained in you. Practice will make it simpler and more effective to mentally perform these actions.

Allow Yourself Some Distance

Taking a step back from strong emotions can help you make sure you're responding to them rationally. Physical separation, such as leaving an unpleasant circumstance, might constitute this distance. But by diverting your attention, you can also establish some mental distance.

It's not healthy to completely block or avoid feelings, but it's also good to divert your attention from them until you're in a better position to deal with them. Please be sure to visit them again. Healthy diversion only lasts for a short time.

Try:

- spending some time with your pet
- going for a walk
- watching a funny video
- chatting with a loved one

Start a Mood Journal

Finding any disruptive patterns might be made easier by writing down your thoughts and feelings and the reactions they elicit. Sometimes, it's sufficient to mentally follow your thoughts back via your emotions. Writing down emotions can help you think about them more thoroughly.

Mental Toughness

It also aids in identifying the situations that lead to emotions that are more difficult to manage, such as difficulties at work or family conflicts. Finding precise triggers enables the development of more effective management techniques.

Journaling every day is most beneficial. Have a journal close by and record strong feelings or emotions as they arise. Try to keep track of your reaction and the triggers. If your response wasn't helpful, use your journal to research further potential solutions that can be beneficial.

Regulate, Don't Suppress

There's no switch to make it easy to regulate your emotions. Just take a moment to imagine that you could control your emotions in this manner. You wouldn't want to leave them constantly operating at full capacity. You wouldn't want to completely turn them off either.

You restrict yourself from feeling and expressing emotions when you suppress or repress them. This may occur intentionally (suppression) or unconsciously (repression).

Both can lead to signs of mental and physical disorders, such as:

- trouble controlling stress
- sleep problems
- muscular spasms and discomfort
- anxiety

- depression

- misuse of substances

Be sure you aren't just brushing your emotions under the rug while trying to gain control over them. It's important to strike a balance between having too many feelings and having none at all for maintaining healthy emotional expression.

See a Professional

If your emotions are still too strong for you to handle, perhaps it's advisable to get some professional help. Several mental health illnesses, including bipolar disorder and borderline personality disorder, are associated with long-term or persistent emotional dysregulation and mood swings.

Having trouble controlling your emotions might also be related to trauma, familial problems, or other underlying difficulties.

A therapist can provide you with sympathetic, nonjudgmental support as you:

- deal with extreme mood swings.

- learn how to control your emotions, either to up-regulate or down-regulate them.

- investigate the causes of poorly controlled emotions.

- practice questioning and rephrasing distressing feelings.

Mood swings and strong emotions might bring on undesirable or negative ideas, which can eventually bring on feelings of helplessness or despair.

This loop may eventually result in unproductive coping mechanisms like self-harm or even suicidal thoughts. Speak to a loved one you can trust if this happens so they can help you gain support immediately.

Coping with stress and strong emotions is often challenging, but it is possible. Cultivate the habits we've discussed in this chapter to help yourself regulate stress and emotions, thereby enhancing your mental toughness.

The impact of self-talk on your inner strength must never be underestimated. Although we have touched on the subject throughout the book, we will focus solely on self-talk in the next chapter.

Luke Thybulle

Chapter 8: Harnessing the Power of Self-Talk

Most of us routinely have a continuous dialogue in our minds. This internal dialogue can take many different forms, such as telling ourselves what to do while carrying out a task, making arbitrary observations about our surroundings or a situation, or engaging in what is frequently referred to as self-talk.

The mental story you tell yourself defines self-talk. It's your inner voice, and you might or might not have given it any thought or attention. Truth be told, we often underestimate the power of our internal dialogue on how we perceive ourselves and the world.

Self-talk is typically understood to be a combination of our conscious and unconscious prejudices and ideas about who we are and the world at large. The notion that we have both conscious and unconscious levels of thinking, with unconscious cognitive processes influencing our behavior in ways we are unaware of, was initially put forth by Sigmund Freud (Cherry, 2022).

Paying attention to your self-talk can help you start making proactive adjustments in how you approach life's obstacles, as self-talk can be either positive or negative.

Luke Thybulle

The Impact of Self-Talk on Mental Toughness

When you have low self-esteem, it is likely that you'll have a negative internal dialogue.

Self-talk can increase or decrease mental toughness for a very simple reason—emotions are directly influenced by our thinking.

Thoughts are linked to specific memories, pictures, and emotions. When we think in a particular way, our minds produce the familiar emotional response.

Thoughts are happening in the background of your mind when you're feeling angry, upset, or glad, even though you might not be aware of them right away. These mental responses are the emotional seeds that you experience.

This process intensifies as thoughts become more direct self-talk.

The thought-feeling cycle is a result of ongoing impressions, which are taking place with each thought.

Once a thought has occurred, an emotional reaction is brought on, which prompts other thoughts. If not immediately impacted, these thoughts will revolve around the same emotion. This is why getting yourself out of a bad mood may be so challenging. Your thoughts feed off one another, and so do your feelings.

The core basis for why self-talk may either boost your mental toughness or send you spiraling downward is thought-driving emotion.

Mental Toughness

Confidence is lowered not only by overtly negative but also by uncertain thoughts. Although these could be considered neutral ideas, in terms of mental toughness, they should be categorized as negative self-talk.

The following instances of prevalent negative self-talk will weaken mental toughness:

- I've been feeling off lately.
- I doubt that I'll be selected for the team.
- I hope I don't mess it up.
- How are we supposed to compete when the other team is so good?
- I cannot make a mistake since it will lower my stats.
- I knew that I wouldn't succeed.
- I'm not that talented.
- I suck.
- I hope they'll like me.

Do you often use such self-talk?

These are all examples of thoughts that will weaken one's mental toughness. Each one brings another emotion other than confidence.

You will fall into the thought-feeling loop if you keep saying these kinds of things to yourself since repetition is what our minds crave. It will be very challenging to progress to a high level of mental toughness from there.

The only way to achieve this is through using constructive self-talk.

Your thoughts produce an emotional state in the same way that they do in other processes. The internal conversation you are having in your head is the only thing that differs.

Constructive self-talk will serve as your personal motivational speaker. It will be taken care of by your own thoughts; you won't need to wait for someone else to encourage you.

It is effective to tell yourself things that will help you develop self-belief. In addition to boosting mental toughness, it will also raise confidence and lessen the dread and worry that fuel self-doubt.

Consider how you interact with those who are close to you. Do you berate someone for making a mistake, telling them how terrible they are and how you knew they couldn't do it? Or, do you use phrases like "Keep your head up" and "That's okay, you'll get them next time" instead? We are so ready to encourage those around us, but we let our own negative self-talk creep in.

Start talking to yourself as though you were your own colleague or friend to boost your self-confidence.

These are some excellent self-talk phrases to use to increase your self-assurance and mental toughness:

- Whatever comes, I'm prepared.

- I am certain of my skills.

- I believe in my abilities.

- Okay, I'll get it next time.

- I want to succeed.

- I have confidence.

- I have faith in myself.

- I can do this.

It's not necessary to use complicated self-talk sentences to boost your mental toughness. In reality, simplicity is best. All you're hoping for is for them to give you a sense of self-confidence.

How to Change Negative Self-Talk to Positive Self-Talk

Positive thinking doesn't involve burying your head in the sand and ignoring life's less-than-ideal circumstances. Simply said, positive thinking entails taking a positive and constructive approach to bad situations. You anticipate the greatest, not the worst, occurrence.

Self-talk is typically the first step in positive thinking. Self-talk is the never-ending stream of inner dialogue that occurs. Positive or negative thoughts may automatically come to mind. Your self-talk contains some elements of logic and reason. Other self-talk may result from false beliefs you make as a consequence of lacking knowledge.

You must develop a positive outlook if you want to succeed in life, whether it is as an entrepreneur or in competitive chess. Our default language toward ourselves is so often negative. Every time we make a small error, we begin to criticize ourselves and have negative thoughts.

And indeed, changing that self-talk from negative to positive is the best mindset you can cultivate.

Here are three methods for switching to more positive self-talk:

Write Down Positive Things You Are Grateful For

Make a list of three positive things as soon as you notice yourself slipping into the negative thought cycle. You can list positives like learning a lesson or understanding yourself better even if you messed up or something went wrong. Gratitude can also help you focus on the positive. Make a mental list of three things for which you are grateful rather than thinking or saying anything bad.

Positive thoughts can train your brain and assist you in avoiding negative self-talk by taking the place of your negative ones. You will eventually be able to recognize when you are doing it and switch your thinking.

Investigate Your Negative Thoughts

Our negative thoughts often attempt to engage with us, prompting our bodies and minds to become defensive. Leaning into the negative thoughts and addressing the reasons behind them can be beneficial. If negativity is being brought on by a fear of failing or losing, deal with the fear as the source of the negativity. Try to overcome the fear instead of shoving bad ideas away.

Picture Yourself Older and Wiser

Imagine a more experienced and mature version of yourself whenever you make a mistake and are tempted to think or say anything negative. What would that more experienced someone say to you? Instead of beating you up, they would probably advise you to keep going and try again. You can get perspective and realize that one error doesn't define your entire life or career by picturing an older version of yourself.

Bad things and mistakes will inevitably occur in your life and profession. The secret to success is not beating yourself up over every tiny error, but rather converting those failures into learning experiences. These techniques can help you think more positively and position you for long-term success.

Luke Thybulle

Everyday Habits for Effective Self-Talk

Your attitude on life is more likely to be negative if the majority of your thoughts are negative. You probably consider yourself an optimist or someone who engages in positive thinking, if your thoughts are generally positive.

Let's talk about habits you can cultivate to keep those thoughts positive! As stated earlier in this chapter, it doesn't mean that we simply disregard all thoughts that appear to be negative. If a thought seems to be anything but positive, pay attention to it, analyze it, and then decide whether the thought will be helpful or not. If not, throw it out.

Be in the Company of Positive People

Make sure the people you surround yourself with are positive, encouraging, and capable of providing insightful feedback. Those who are negative might make you feel more stressed out and make you doubt your capacity to handle stress in healthy ways.

Stop and Evaluate

Stop periodically throughout the day to assess your thoughts. Try to find a way to reframe your thinking if you notice your thoughts are primarily negative.

Adopt a Healthy Lifestyle

On the majority of the days of the week, try to complete at least 30 minutes of exercise. It can also be divided into 10-minute intervals throughout the day. Stress reduction and mood improvement are two benefits of exercise. Eat well to nourish both your body and mind, and acquire stress management skills. What you eat can greatly impact your mood. Eating healthy foods will help you have a clear mind and think positive thoughts.

Determine What Needs to Change

If you want to think more positively and be more optimistic, start by identifying the aspects of your life that you tend to negatively focus on, such as work, a relationship, or your daily commute. By concentrating on one subject, you can begin small and tackle it more positively.

Embrace Humor

Give yourself permission to laugh or smile, especially when things are tough. Find humor in commonplace events. You feel less stressed when you can laugh at life. However, maintain a balance, you don't want to make a joke out of everything. We all occasionally face serious matters when humor would be inappropriate. Therefore, seek out things that you can add a humorous twist to. See this as an adventurous challenge.

Engage in Positive Self-Talk

Always consider this one simple rule: Never say anything to yourself that you wouldn't say to your best friend. Be kind and supportive of yourself. When a negative thought arises, analyze it logically and counter it by focusing on your positive traits. Consider the aspects of your life for which you are grateful.

Here are some examples of negative self-talk and how you can turn it into positive:

Negative Self-Talk	**Giving It a Positive Spin**
Nobody bothers to get in touch with me.	I'll try to get the lines of communication open.
I am too lazy to complete this.	There was no place for it in my schedule, but I can re-evaluate some of my priorities.
I've never done this before.	It's a chance to gain new skills and information.
The change is too drastic.	Let's take a chance.
I lack the resources to achieve it.	The invention process is driven by necessity.

Mental Toughness

That won't work in any way.	I can try and make it work.
It's too difficult.	I'll approach it from a different perspective.
I won't become any more adept at this.	I'll attempt it once again.

To become more aware of your self-talk, begin writing it down. Every time you catch your inner voice talking down to you, write down exactly what came into your mind in a similar way as the example above. Then, see if you can add your own positive twist to it. It's a very effective way to change the habit of negative self-talk. Many people have become so accustomed to it that they started to believe that negative inner voice. But you don't have to. You can, and should, change it!

Expecting to become an optimist overnight is unrealistic if you have a tendency to be negative. Yet over time, you'll become less critical of yourself and more accepting of who you are. You can also start to lose your sense of self-criticism.

Being ever-optimistic makes it easier for you to deal with daily stress more beneficially. Such an ability could be a factor in positive thinking's well-documented health advantages.

There is indeed power in self-talk. The good thing about self-talk is that it is about yourself—no one else can choose how you do it. This means that, if you want to become more positive, confident,

Luke Thybulle

and have unwavering mental toughness, you can work on your self-talk and change it for good.

So, first, choose to be kind to yourself. Then, be conscious of your self-talk. If it is unkind, stop it, and change it. You can do it! You are on your way to a world of innovation, success, and fulfillment!

Conclusion

We all inherently wish to improve our circumstances in some way. In every circumstance, we strive for greater happiness, joy, and pleasure.

You are acting in accordance with your goal-oriented mentality when you go after your ambitions. When you are not pursuing worthwhile goals, you are acting against your nature and experiencing unresolved discontent. Moreover, success advances us toward a greater self.

The next phase of your progress is represented by your current ambitions. If you want to get to the next stage of your development right now, you must evolve into a person deserving of your goals in order to fulfill them.

You need to be a highly-skilled, results-oriented individual to succeed in your career. To succeed financially, find opportunities to serve others so your thoughts translate healthily regarding material possessions. Succeeding in relationships requires you to sincerely love people, expressed through compassion, understanding, and generosity.

Success is the opposite of failure. The majority of human suffering is caused by not achieving our fundamental goals. You doubt your capacity as a human being every time you fail with a person or a goal. You experience mistrust, bitterness, and rage. You lose confidence when you keep losing.

This is why success is important. It is about developing into the type of person who can achieve your most important goals. Our capacity for evolution is what determines our self-esteem, including our mental toughness.

In Chapter 1, we examined mental toughness and found that people today realize that skill alone cannot guarantee success. Mental toughness serves as both a performance enhancer and a critical factor in obtaining performance excellence. The significance of psychological intervention and its effects on performance are still worrisomely underappreciated.

Our capacity to appropriately balance internal and external demands will determine whether we experience positive or negative emotional reactions in response to challenging situations or other types of adversity, as well as the effects these reactions have on our productivity. Our mental toughness contributes to the outcome, not our circumstances.

We can fight off negative thoughts by being mentally tough. We can regularly re-enter the ups and downs of life thanks to it. Like working out muscles for physical strength, we may develop this type of mental muscle to improve our overall well-being.

In Chapter 2, we talked about resilience and how it is related to inner strength. Resilience can be referred to as the "immune system" of the mind and psyche. While some individuals are naturally gifted with high levels of emotional resilience, others must first develop and practice this ability.

Resilient people are regarded as being positive, solution-focused, adaptable, and imaginative. They can quickly recover from losses, control stress and challenges, and take advantage of opportunities when they present themselves. Some traits of people with good resilience include constantly thinking of possibilities and knowing how to solve difficulties efficiently.

The terms "mental toughness" and "mental resilience" are not synonymous. It can be characterized as a personality trait that, regardless of the circumstance, has a significant impact on how someone will respond mentally to pressure, chance, and challenge. A person with mental toughness views difficulty and adversity as an opportunity rather than a danger, and they have the self-assurance and optimistic outlook to take whatever comes their way.

Thus, there is a link between mental toughness and mental resilience. Most, if not all, mentally tough people are mentally resilient, but not all mentally resilient people are mentally tough. The distinguishing factor is the positive element. We also talked about the pillars of resilience and habits to cultivate for improving resilience.

In Chapter 3, we discussed limiting beliefs and how they impact your life, as well as the benefits of adopting a growth mindset. Because our results are limited by our unconscious beliefs, we keep falling short of our boundless potential. Limiting beliefs have an effect on all facets of our lives and can cause us difficulty in a variety of ways. We naturally focus our efforts primarily on activities we believe will provide the outcomes we desire.

As a result, when we are hesitant because we believe something won't work out, even unintentionally, we negate our potential. Inaction yields subpar outcomes. Bad outcomes translate to uncertainty and demoralized beliefs. That is a vicious cycle that can only be ended by changing your input.

Ways to change our limiting beliefs include accepting responsibility, letting go of certainty, determining what our limiting beliefs are, and to stop worrying about what other people think of us. We must also let go of entitled beliefs and decide not to be content with less-than-ideal circumstances.

While a fixed mindset keeps us locked in our comfort zones, a growth mindset is set on learning, growing, and improving. A fixed mindset believes that you can only use your current skills and knowledge, while a growth mindset understands that new skills can be acquired. Cultivating habits for establishing and maintaining a growth mindset will strengthen your mind and aid in enhancing your mental toughness.

In Chapter 4, we explored the benefits of positive thinking. Positive thinking enables you to overcome obstacles without being anxious. Additionally, you don't become upset when you don't get something you desire. Also, even if something unexpected occurs that you didn't want, you still feel good about it. With your continual optimism, you inspire everyone around you. You serve as a source of inspiration and motivation for others.

You enjoy recognizing other people's accomplishments. Regardless of your current situation, you have optimism for the future. You always compliment someone on a job well done when they do something good. Whether it's a toddler or an adult, you like brightening someone's day. No matter how unfair your situation seems to you, you never complain.

To enjoy a positive mindset, eliminate negative thoughts. Cognitive distortions warp reality, making you believe that things are far worse than they are. Or it can lean towards the other extreme—that you don't recognize the seriousness or impact of something. Habits for improving a positive mindset include using positive affirmations, staying in the present, and accepting the things that you cannot change.

In Chapter 5, we covered setting achievable goals. In the long run, setting goals will lead to greater success and fulfillment in all areas of your life. Setting goals has many benefits. Regularly achieving your goals will keep you motivated and moving in the direction of your aspirations. Goal failure, however, can harm confidence. This is only one of many reasons why setting reasonable goals is so important.

By tracking your daily progress and making the required adjustments, you can keep your focus and build good goal-setting habits. If you didn't manage to complete tasks you had planned, consider how you may concentrate more on your goals tomorrow. Achieving your target is a cause for celebration. When you reach a goal, don't be reluctant to reward yourself.

In Chapter 6, we discussed emotional intelligence. Emotional intelligence, also known as emotional quotient (EQ), is the capacity to identify, use, and regulate your own emotions in order to lower stress, communicate properly, sympathize with others, overcome challenges, and diffuse conflict. With the help of emotional intelligence, you can strengthen your relationships, perform effectively at work and school, and accomplish your professional and personal goals. Also, it can help you connect with your emotions, carry out your intentions, and decide what is most essential to you.

Emotional intelligence has four constructs:

- self-awareness

- relationship management

- self-management

- social awareness

It affects many areas of your life, including relationships, academic or professional performance, and your physical and mental well-being. Emotional intelligence is a key aspect of mental toughness. You cannot be internally fortified if you lack the ability to fully recognize, accept, and act upon severely negative feelings. Your emotional intelligence will finally be put to the test by situations that will challenge your mental toughness.

In Chapter 7, we saw that it is essential to manage stress and emotions. Stress can motivate people and is sometimes required for survival. The body's fight-or-flight response mechanism teaches a person when and how to respond to danger. Yet, if the body is too readily triggered or when there are too many stresses present at once, it may have an impact on a person's physical and mental health.

You might be able to regulate your emotions without suppressing or dominating them. You can use this to improve your relationships, attitude, decision-making, and mental toughness. Habits to regulate your emotions include keeping stress under control, knowing when you can express yourself freely, and accepting and acknowledging all your emotions before dealing with them.

In Chapter 8, we discussed the power of self-talk. Most of us regularly engage in an ongoing mental conversation. This inner dialogue can appear in a variety of ways, including instructing ourselves what to do while carrying out a task, making arbitrary judgments about our environment or a situation, or participating in what is usually referred to as self-talk.

Self-talk is the narrative that one convinces themselves of. You may or may not have given your inner voice any thought or attention. The truth is that we frequently underestimate the influence of our internal conversations on how we view the world and ourselves. Negative self-talk can greatly harm mental toughness.

Self-talk can affect mental toughness positively or negatively for the very clear reason that our emotions are influenced by our thoughts. Thoughts are connected to particular emotions, images, and memories. Our thoughts create a familiar emotional response when we think in a specific way.

Even though you might not be immediately aware of them, while you're furious, upset, or happy, thoughts are still occurring in the backdrop of your mind. Your emotional experiences are sparked by these mental reactions.

As self-talk in the mind becomes blunter, this process becomes more intense.

The continuing impressions that occur with each thought are what lead to the thought-feeling cycle. This means, to improve mental toughness, we need to feed ourselves with constructive thoughts and words—positive self-talk.

Luke Thybulle

How do you feel about yourself? Is there room for change? Don't be afraid. Implement the habits provided in this book, and witness your life change. You now have enough tools, tips, tricks, and strategies to make a world's difference, not only for yourself, but also for those you respect, cherish, and love.

If you found this book to be inspirational, helpful, or life-changing (hopefully all of these!), kindly leave a positive review so I am enabled to reach more people. The world needs us! Let's step up and help those who need it!

FREE E-Book:
Discover How to Finally Conquer Your Fears

PLUS I'll share with you
My #1 Secret To Guaranteed Success...
See firsthand how I direct my focus to live a life full of energy, passion and confidence.

- Luke Thybulle

www.northstarreaders.com/luke-thybulle/conquer-your-fears

Luke Thybulle

References

Ackerman, C. E. (2018, July 5). *Positive mindset: How to develop a positive mental attitude.* PositivePsychology.com. https://positivepsychology.com/positive-mindset/

Anderson, J. (2023, February 24). *20 small habits that will help you become mentally strong.* LifeHack. https://www.lifehack.org/354489/20-small-habits-build-become-mentally-stronger-this-year

Bradberry, T., & Greaves, J. (2009). *Emotional intelligence 2.0.* Talentsmart.

Brown, L. L. (2008). *The courage to win: A revolutionary mental toughness formula: How to master yourself to make more money, fast track your career and win in love.* Lisa Brown & Associates.

Chapman, M. (2016). *50 positive habits: Transform you life: The art of marginal gains.* Personality Development Mastery.

Cherry, K. (2022a, August 15). *The life, work, and theories of Sigmund Freud.* Verywell Mind; Verywellmind. https://www.verywellmind.com/sigmund-freud-his-life-work-and-theories-2795860

Cherry, K. (2022b, November 7). *What is emotional intelligence?* Verywell Mind.

https://www.verywellmind.com/what-is-emotional-intelligence-2795423

Cooks-Campbell, A. (2022, June 2). *When tough isn't enough, build mental strength. Here's how.* BetterUp. https://www.betterup.com/blog/mental-strength

Cowan, W. (2023, February 21). *"Bloom from where you are."* Medium. https://medium.com/@wendycowan/bloom-from-where-you-are-7fd8578460c5

Dagher, K. (2022, May 27). *10 steps to creating a plan to achieve your goals.* Fellow. https://fellow.app/blog/productivity/steps-to-creating-a-plan-to-achieve-your-goals/

De Bono, E. (2018). *Future positive: Change your mindset for a positive future.* Vermilion.

Divine, M. (2015). *Unbeatable mind: Forging mental toughness.* Mark D Divine.

Dutton, V. (2015, May 22). *Seven growth mindset habits for success.* Planet Positive Change. https://planetpositivechange.com/seven-growth-mindset-habits-for-success/

Dweck, C. S. (2016). *Mindset: The new psychology of success: How we can learn to fulfill our potential.* Random House.

Eatough, E. (2022, May 13). *10 tips to set goals and achieve them.* BetterUp. https://www.betterup.com/blog/how-to-set-goals-and-achieve-them#

Felman, A. (2020, March 12). *Why stress happens and how to manage it.* MedicalNewsToday. https://www.medicalnewstoday.com/articles/145855#definition

Flaxington, B. (2013). *Self-Talk for a calmer you: Learn how to use positive self-talk to control anxiety and live a happier, more relaxed life.* Adams Media.

Goleman, D. (2009). *Emotional intelligence: Why it can matter more than IQ.* Bloomsbury Publishing.

Greenberg, M. (2017). *The stress-proof brain: Master your emotional response to stress using mindfulness & neuroplasticity.* New Harbinger Publications.

Halvorson, C. (2015, October 12). *11 habits of people who always reach their goals.* Insider. https://www.businessinsider.com/11-habits-of-people-who-always-reach-their-goals-2015-10

Humphreys, J. (2021, January 18). *What is mental resilience?* Redefining Communications. https://redefiningcomms.com/what-is-mental-resilience/

Jerus, R. (2018, August 14). *Emotional intelligence of mental toughness.* LinkedIn. https://www.linkedin.com/pulse/emotional-intelligence-mental-toughness-robert/

Lin, Y., Mutz, J., Clough, P. J., & Papageorgiou, K. A. (2017). Mental toughness and individual differences in learning, educational and work performance, psychological well-being, and personality: A systematic review. *Sec. Personality and Social Psychology, 8*. https://doi.org/10.3389/fpsyg.2017.01345

Lindenberger, B. (2021, September 24). *7 daily habits to build your resilience*. Success. https://www.success.com/7-daily-habits-to-build-your-resilience/

Lupien, S. (2012). *Well stressed: Manage stress before it turns toxic*. John Wiley & Sons.

Mallory, P. (2021, June 15). *The effect of stress and pressure on your people*. LinkedIn. https://www.linkedin.com/pulse/effect-stress-pressure-your-people-penny-mallory/

Marteka. (2019, July 15). *12 ways to recognise negative thoughts*. Benevolent Health. https://benevolenthealth.co.uk/12-ways-to-recognise-negative-thoughts/

Mayo Clinic Staff. (2021, March 18). *Stress relievers: Tips to tame stress*. Mayo Clinic. https://www.mayoclinic.org/healthy-lifestyle/stress-management/in-depth/stress-relievers/art-20047257#

Mayo Clinic Staff. (2022, February 3). *Positive thinking: Stop negative self-talk to reduce stress*. Mayo Clinic. https://www.mayoclinic.org/healthy-lifestyle/stress-management/in-depth/positive-thinking/art-20043950

Mead, E. (2019, September 26). *What is positive self-talk? (Incl. examples)*. PositivePsychology.com. https://positivepsychology.com/positive-self-talk/

Meadows, M. (2015). *Confidence: How to overcome your limiting beliefs and achieve your goals*. Meadows Publishing.

Meadows, M. (2017a). *365 days with self-discipline: 365 life-altering thoughts on self-control, mental resilience, and success*. Meadows Publishing.

Meadows, M. (2017b). *From failure to success: Everyday habits and exercises to build mental resilience and turn failures into successes*. Meadows Publishing.

Meadows, M. (2017c). *The ultimate focus strategy: How to set the right goals, develop powerful focus, stick to the process, and achieve success*. Meadows Publishing.

Morgan, J. (2020, December 15). *3 strategies to move from negative to positive thinking*. Medium. https://medium.com/jacob-morgan/3-strategies-to-move-from-negative-to-positive-thinking-a892d6d8536e

Pattison, S. (2013, May 24). *What is mental toughness and why do you need it?* Believe Perform. https://believeperform.com/what-is-mental-toughness-and-why-do-you-need-it/

PurposeFairy.com. (2022, June 16). *4 essential habits of positive people to inspire and empower you*. The Epoch Times. https://www.theepochtimes.com/4-essential-habits-of-positive-people-to-inspire-and-empower-you_4537580.html?welcomeuser=1

Raypole, C. (2020, April 28). *How to become the boss of your emotions*. Healthline.

https://www.healthline.com/health/how-to-control-your-emotions#therapy

Regenesys Business School. (2021, October 27). *13 thoughts on mental toughness.* RegInsights. https://www.regenesys.net/reginsights/13-thoughts-on-mental-toughness/

Ridsdel, J. (2021, April 1). *10 common negative thinking patterns and 5 steps for change.* The Family Centre. https://www.familycentre.org/news/post/10-common-negative-thinking-patterns-and-5-steps-for-change

Robbins, T. (2021a, September 20). *The complete guide to limiting beliefs.* Robbins Research International, Inc. https://www.tonyrobbins.com/limiting-beliefs-guide/

Robbins, T. (2021b, September 23). *How to overcome your limiting beliefs.* Robbins Research International, Inc. https://www.tonyrobbins.com/limiting-beliefs-guide/overcoming-limiting-beliefs/

Rosie. (2014, September 17). *The loneliness of mental health problems.* Mind. https://www.mind.org.uk/information-support/your-stories/the-loneliness-of-mental-health-problems/

Satterwhite, A. K. (2016). *Understanding mental toughness and stress: The role of Cortisol.* https://scholarship.rollins.edu/cgi/viewcontent.cgi?article=1035&context=honors#

Schuy, M. (2022, March 8). *Factors of resilience – 7 skills to master the art of resilience.* CleverMemo. https://clevermemo.com/blog/en/factors-of-resilience/

Segal, J., Smith, M., Robinson, L., & Shubin, J. (2020, October). *Improving emotional intelligence (EQ).* HelpGuide.org. https://www.helpguide.org/articles/mental-health/emotional-intelligence-eq.htm#

Siebold, S. (2010). *177 mental toughness secrets of the world class: The thought processes, habits and philosophies of the great ones.* London House.

Sparks, D. (2019, May 29). *Mayo mindfulness: Overcoming negative self-talk.* Mayo Clinic. https://newsnetwork.mayoclinic.org/discussion/mayo-mindfulness-overcoming-negative-self-talk/

Straw, E. (2023, March 14). *The impact self-talk has on your confidence.* Success Starts Within. https://www.successstartswithin.com/blog/the-impact-self-talk-has-on-your-confidence

Strycharczyk, D. (2021, June 23). *Resilience and mental toughness–Is there a difference and does it matter?* AQR International. https://aqrinternational.co.uk/resilience-and-mental-toughness-is-there-a-difference-and-does-it-matter

Tracy, B. (2019, September 6). *Goal setting – your guide to setting and achieving goals.* Brian Tracy International. https://www.briantracy.com/blog/personal-success/goal-setting/

Why mindset is important in life? (2022, October 8). Selfpause. https://selfpause.com/mindset/why-mindset-is-important-in-life/

Wilson, S. B., & Dobson, M. S. (2008). *Goal setting: How to create an action plan and achieve your goals.* American Management Association.

Wright, H. N. (2011). *A better way to think: Using positive thoughts to change your life.* Revell.

Printed in Great Britain
by Amazon

efcdf5bb-f65d-4e33-ad98-788a3f8d3194R01